PROMISING PRACTICES

Prekindergarten
MUSIC EDUCATION

PROMISING PRACTICES

Prekindergarten
MUSIC EDUCATION

Edited by Barbara Andress

MENC MENC
MENC MENC
The National Association for Music Education

Cover photos by Peter Berglund and ASU Media Production

DISCARD

TABLE OF CONTENTS

Foreword

by Barbara Andress

As the demand for prekindergarten educational programs increases in the nation, music educators are looking for ways to make music a significant and important part of these experiences. In recent years, professional organizations and other in-service sponsors have provided us with opportunities to attend workshops, seminars, and special classes where the topic dealt with music for young children. Session leaders have shared ideas about child development, musical behaviors, and materials that may be appropriately used with very young children.

Several books are now on the market that provide insight as to how one might shape the learning environment for this age group. It now seems appropriate to ask, "How are we doing?" Has the information about young children and music been put into practice? What kinds of programs are being fielded, explored, or tested? Are there designs and administrative strategies for such programs? Do any of the models merit replication in other settings? Are there any promising practices out there?

Music educators are implementing programs in research-oriented settings, as commercial enterprises, and in public school systems. We must begin to share information about how some of these programs are going about the business of musically educating young children or preparing the adults who are working with these youngsters.

The material in this book attempts to identify some of the promising practices that exist in the area of early childhood education. The introductory article sets the philosophical stance reiterated in many of the articles: "Play is the young child's most viable method of learning." The articles continue by providing descriptive information about (1) university-based early childhood music programs, in which the elements of research and teacher preparation are often inherent factors; (2) commercial programs that have been developed by talented, concerned individuals; and (3) prekindergarten programs in the public school, in which music educators have met the challenge of suddenly enacted legislative mandates.

Part four describes some additional promising practices that deal with specific ideas such as challenging undergraduates to create developmentally appropriate materials for prekindergarten learning centers, factors in setting music and movement environments, and activities that motivate creative thinking in prekindergarten children. Planners will find such information most helpful when making decisions about program development.

The authors of the articles have described their programs in their own unique ways. In some instances, the authors' writing style reflects the poetic and creative talents of the program originators. Some authors have elected to provide a comprehensive look at the overall program, while others have chosen to focus on the specific content of their sessions with children and have included useful songs and activities.

These promising practices are but a few of the many fine programs that exist throughout the country. Educators who wish to become involved in the research and development of programs for very young children will do well to search out model programs in their own geographic areas, as well as to synthesize and adapt ideas from this collection.

PLAY AND MUSIC can be joined, forming a pathway to learning for the young child. Opportunities for developmentally appropriate music play, using both teacher-directed and child-initiated experiences, should be included in preschool classrooms.

Introduction

Child's Play: Pathways to Music Learning

by Danette Littleton

Twelve four-year-olds enter the familiar music room eager and chattering delightedly: "I want the big drum..." "Will you play the violin with me?" The children scatter throughout the music room already prepared with an eclectic arrangement of musical instruments and props such as the baton and hand-held microphones, Miss Piggy, Kermit, and other puppet friends. The visitor asks the music teacher, "When does this lesson begin?" "This is the lesson," the teacher replies. "They have come to play...."

Play has not received high marks from some authorities charged with the education of children. It is often viewed as a wasteful, even harmful activity that impedes the serious business of preparing children for adulthood and work. Even the phrase "child's play" denotes disdain for the trivial and insignificant. The philosophy that child's play is unimportant has been challenged over time, however, by powerful voices.

In the eighteenth century, it was Froebel who placed play in the center of child development: "Play is the highest expression of what is in a child's soul" (Frost and Sunderlin 1985). In the twentieth century, Piaget embraced child's play in his cognitive-developmental model of how children learn. Piaget showed that the child's thinking styles influence the nature and complexity of play from infancy. An artistic view of child's play is expressed by Frost and Sunderlin (1985, ix):

> Portraits of the child at play represent the innate potentialities in human beings to seek and to express themselves—artistically, freely, creatively, and thus to gain fulfillment. Play is the child's art form, the vehicle for creative expression, the primary avenue to learning and development, a source of joy and contentment.

In the experiences of children, the art of play and the art of music merge to provide a unique pathway to learning. Many of the present practices in prekindergarten music education are based on the supposition that music learning best occurs through circle-time song singing, pantomiming and moving to musical recordings, and playing along with music on rhythm instruments. Such music experiences are selected and directed by the teacher, while the children participate in a manner much like playing games with rules...adult rules. Another

CONTACT: *Danette Littleton, University of Tennessee at Chattanooga, Department of Music, Chattanooga, TN 37403* approach to music learning for young children is through the child's pathway, his or her natural ability to play. To better understand the role of children's play in musical development, teachers can turn once again to the work of Jean Piaget.

Piaget explains play within the context of the child's cognitive structure. He believes that it is the nature of the child that his or her cognitive structure will lead to play. In *Play, Dreams and Imitation in Childhood*, Piaget distinguished three major categories of play: practice play, symbolic play, and games with rules; reflecting the sensorimotor, preoperational, and concrete operational stages of development. He wrote:

> While mere practice play begins with the first months of life and symbolic play during the second year, games with rules rarely occur before stage two (ages 4–7) and belong mainly to the third period (ages 7–11) (Piaget 1962, 142).

Smilansky (1968, 5–7) redefined and expanded Piaget's cognitive play categories and provides teachers with a guide for observing and examining children's play:

> *Functional play*. Initially, the play of children consists of simple muscular activities based on the need for physical action. Children repeat actions and manipulations, imitate themselves, try new actions, imitate them and continuously engage in the action/imitation cycle.
>
> *Constructive play*. This form of play provides children opportunities to create. Children move from functional activity to activity that results in a "creation." From the *sporadic* handling of sand or bricks, children move to *building* something from these materials that can remain after play has ended.
>
> *Dramatic play*. Children take on roles: They pretend to be somebody or something else. While doing this they draw from their first- or second-hand experiences with other people in different situations. They imitate other people, in action and speech, with the aid of real or imagined objects.
>
> *Games with rules*. Children learn to accept prearranged rules and to adjust to them. More important, they learn to control behavior, actions, and reactions within time limits.

Reflection on these stages of children's play reveals that most music education programs for young children fail to provide developmentally appropriate opportunities for music play. Children learn rote songs, follow prescribed movements, and play music and singing games. Many of these activities, routinely accepted in the preschool classroom with three- and four-year-olds, best fit the final and most complex stage of developmental play—games with rules. For, to sing and move to music appropriately, children must learn to accept and adjust to prearranged rules and learn to control behaviors, actions, and reactions in the determined time limits. Further, the temporal aspect of music requires a sophisticated concept of musical time that places even greater demands on the young player.

This is not to suggest that free-play music activities should replace the traditional music program for young children, rather that opportunities for developmentally appropriate music play be included in preschool classrooms. A balance of teacher-directed and child-initiated music experiences is central to an educationally sound music program for children before the age of seven. Andress (1980) described a child-centered music curriculum that recognizes the importance of child-initiated experiences, teacher-directed group activities, and teacher-guided activities with individual children and small groups of children:

> Our traditional approach, involving children in large settings where they listen, play, sing, and move to heritage music materials, can no longer represent the sole part of a larger program in which children interact and make decisions about sounds, their quality, intensity, pitch, and duration. The children should manipulate and play with sounds, musical and environmental, as a means to ordering and organizing their musical world (Andress 1980, 3).

Investigation of Andress's concept of a child-centered music curriculum and Piaget's developmental model of the role of children's play leads to a third source of information on preschool children's musical play: the Pillsbury studies. Although few studies have been conducted on free play and music, these particularly significant studies of preschool children's spontaneous play with music were conducted at the Pillsbury School from 1937 to 1949. In *Music of Young Children,* a report on the school's philosophy and practices, the directors, Gladys Moorhead and Donald Pond, described the music learning environment:

> The musical materials were available exactly as were any other materials, such as blocks, paints, playhouse, and climbing equipment. They were constantly present, were used informally at any time, and most of them could be taken to any spot in the building, porches, or yard where they were wanted. There was no music period and there was no formal music group at any time. There was no restriction to the production of sound except where instruments were misused or during lunch and rest period. There was no attempt to limit vocal production (Moorhead and Pond 1941, 8).

The freedom to explore music, as an individual or with peers, subject to a minimum of adult intervention, characterized this child-centered approach to music learning at the Pillsbury School. Moorhead and Pond also studied the social interactions and the environment in relation to the preschool children's spontaneous music activities:

> Emphasis was placed upon freedom for the children and upon development of social understanding and responsibility, which would give them power to maintain their own activities and organizations with the minimum of adult intervention. This was considered essential, as it was obvious that music as an individual and social activity could reach its natural forms only if the individuals and social groups within the school were free to evolve their own forms (Moorhead and Pond 1941, 8).

The inquisitive Pillsbury School approach to music education for children ages two through six asked a simple question: Do children have a musical culture all their own? Moorhead and Pond posited that since there had been and are many diverse world musical cultures throughout time and around the globe, it might be that the young child in twentieth-century America could have a musical culture specifically his or her own, "as different from that of his adult contemporaries as theirs is from those of the eleventh-century Norman or today's Balinese (music)" (Moorhead and Pond 1941, 2). Nearly fifty years later, the question of a unique children's music culture remains unanswered yet intriguing. The following description provides one view of a group of four-year-old children engaging in musical play of their own making.

The children participating in this music education project were enrolled daily in a preschool program that included a traditional music program. This program provided opportunities for singing heritage songs by rote, moving and singing with recorded music emphasizing basic skills (colors, shapes, numbers, and letters of the alphabet), and using classroom rhythm instruments to accompany recorded music. These group music activities were directed by the teacher during circle-time each morning.

The transition from this traditional teacher-directed program to one that included teacher-guided and child-initiated or free-play activities with music was developed in three stages. First, during the teacher-directed sessions, music experiences were designed to nurture individual musical exploration and play. Attention to novel materials for young children's visual, tactile, and aural experiences with music guided and prompted subsequent play. Second, time was scheduled for teacher-guided music activities. Following each fifteen- to twenty-minute session guided by the teacher, ten minutes of guided play with musical instruments, materials, and manipulatives was provided. Third, child-initiated free play sessions were scheduled separately from the circle-time, teacher-directed music sessions. This special time created opportunities for the children to play freely with music without directions and suggestions from the teacher. The music play environment, containing a variety of music instruments and materials, encouraged spontaneous, creative, and active music play.

In the teacher-directed sessions, developmental music activities were created to emphasize vocal and instrumental sound experiences, to stimulate interest, and to encourage individual children to experiment with sounds. For example, small, hand-held windmills were used by the children to make the sound and sight of the wind as they discovered longer and shorter variations of sounds, "talking drums" of various sizes were played to represent loud and soft-spoken characters in a story, and brightly illustrated music books with large notes were used to encourage children's spontaneous song-making. A period of open-ended activities followed these sessions. In this period, children used engaging materials, often to recreate bits of the previous experiences during guided and free-play time. In the first few minutes, children usually attended to the instruments and props used during the directed activities, after which they turned to explore other materials and classroom instruments. Since there were multiples of each instrument or item, the children required little supervision.

The sequence of musical experience described thus far took the child from teacher-directed to teacher-guided activities to child-initiated activities. The third stage of this project culminated in children's music play for twenty to thirty minutes, free of adult intervention. These music play experiences were observed to be pleasurable, active, spontaneous, and serious business. There were examples of random sound-making with instruments and voices such as chants and sing-song conversations with puppets. Individual children, seemingly playing alone with an instrument, often imitated a rhythm pattern played by another child on the other side of the playroom. Frequently, two children created a call and response musical conversation, taking turns playing on the same or similar instruments while others used "singing" puppets to create story-dramas. Props such as hand-held microphones were used by some children for roles as singing and dancing "rock stars," while the conductor's baton served to "lead" the group. (During one play session, the "conductor" kept repeating with great frustration, "You're not watching me!")

A closer examination of these play experiences yields evidences of functional, constructive, and dramatic play with music. Just as these established categories help inform the educator about the child's emerging cognitive development, they also reveal the child's musical development. Child's play is a pathway to learning, especially music learning. Robert Frost must have understood children as well as poets when he wrote, "An aesthetic experience begins with delight and leads to wisdom."

While there is no exact definition of play, some agreed-upon characteristics that guided this project are important for those who teach music to young children. These are: (1) Play is a source of pleasure, for when drudgery or boredom sets in, play no longer exists; (2) play is spontaneous; (3) play is purposeless—it has no goals outside itself, but exists as play for play's sake; (4) play is active; (5) play is serious—it is child's work; (6) play is self-initiated, for when adults step in to direct, play ceases; and (7) play is learning—it nurtures cognitive, physical, social, affective, and emotional development (Frost and Klein 1983, 21).

A teacher's own memories of childhood play and music may be the greatest source for teachers who would provide children with opportunities to genuinely play with music. How did you respond to music, to sounds, or to instruments you found or created? Did you make story-dramas with singers and dancers? Artur Rubenstein, the great concert pianist, richly recalled his earliest music memories this way:

> My first musical impressions were formed by the lugubrious, plaintive shrieks of factory sirens, hundreds of them waking the workers at six in the morning when the city was still dark. Soon I was offered more pleasant musical fare, when gypsies would appear in the courtyard of our house, singing and dancing with their little dressed-up monkeys, while the singsong of Jewish old-clothes peddlers, of Russian ice cream sellers, and Polish peasant women chanting the praises of their eggs, vegetables, and fruit. I loved all

these noises, and while nothing would induce me to utter a single word, I was always willing to sing—to imitate with my voice—any sound I heard, thus creating quite a sensation at home. This sensation soon degenerated into sport, everyone trying to teach me some songs. In this manner I learned to recognize people by their tunes (Rubenstein 1973, 4).

As it was among the adults in Rubenstein's family, it is our own playfulness that links the child within each of us to the child we teach: the feeling child, the thinking and reasoning child, the creative child, the compassionate child. All of these are a whole fabric woven of the unending thread of play.

References

Andress, B. A. 1980. *Music experiences in early childhood*. New York: Holt, Rinehart and Winston.

Frost, J. L., and B. L. Klein. 1983. *Children's play and playgrounds*. Austin, TX: Playscapes International.

Frost, J. L., and S. Sunderlin. eds. 1985. *When children play*. Wheaton, MD: Association for Childhood Education International.

Moorhead, G., and D. Pond. 1941. *Music of Young Children*. Santa Barbara: Pillsbury Foundation for the Advancement of Music Education.

Piaget, J. 1962. *Play, dreams and imitation in childhood*. New York: Knopf.

Rubenstein, A. 1973. *My young years*. New York: Knopf.

Smilansky, S. 1968. *The effects of sociodramatic play on disadvantaged children: Pre-school children*. New York: Wiley.

Danette Littleton is professor of music at the University of Tennessee at Chattanooga. She has been a successful general music teacher at the public school and university levels. She has presented early childhood workshop sessions at national music educators' meetings in Canada and the United States. She works extensively with prekindergarten children as a part of her ongoing research activities.

The Music Experience Laboratory at the University of Arizona provides young children with opportunities to explore music and provides music educators with an environment in which they can gather data regarding the musical learning processes and musical characteristics of young children. Programs of this type may be set up in church or community centers to teach classes of up to thirty-five children (who attend in the company of their parents), divided into two age groups: children from eighteen months to three years of age, and children from three to five years old.

CHAPTER 1

The Music Experience Laboratory: A Model

by David G. Woods

E arly experiences in sound exploration and movement are essential to creating a foundation for future musical development and growth. Such experiences, when sequenced within the structure of a laboratory situation or when approached informally, create opportunities for building musical vocabulary and skills that will contribute to musical literacy and musical appreciation later in life. The Music Experience Laboratory at the University of Arizona offers an exploratory musical environment for children eighteen months to five years of age to sing, move, and explore sounds in a flexible yet structured environment. The Laboratory also provides a research environment for early childhood music educators who are gathering data regarding musical learning processes of young children and the musical characteristics of young children. A variety of teaching techniques and musical materials are tested, and evaluations are made regarding their effectiveness for musical learning. The following suggestions are made for teachers, parents, and students who wish to establish a music experience laboratory for preschool-age children.

IDEAL SIZE AND SCOPE

Recent research clearly indicates that musical experiences at a very early age have lasting benefits for the children involved (E. Gordon 1984). A music experience laboratory should, therefore, include very young children if possible. The most valuable program design is one that includes a laboratory session for eighteen-month-old to three-year-old children and a session for those who are three to five years of age. The first session, for younger children, will of course focus on experiences and perceptions, while the second session with older preschoolers will extend the experiences and perceptions into preconceptual musical structures. Both sessions are important to an overall program of early childhood music education.

The learning experiences in a laboratory are based on (1) free exploratory activities involving random interaction with sound-making sources in a prepared play area; (2) structured music-and-movement play in which the teacher plans and directs the experiences; and (3) activities directed toward building musical performance skills such as beatkeeping and pitch matching.

The sessions for eighteen-month-old to three-year-old children include movement activities and a fast-paced presentation of songs sung by teachers and parents. Children in this session

CONTACT: David G. Woods, University of Arizona, School of Music, Tucson, AZ 85721 often observe the activities rather than participate in them, but the children are perceiving the musical play and will someday imitate or modify that play in their own worlds of experience.

The sessions for three- to five-year-old children include songs and play with movements that can be imitated and repeated. Many sound-making exploratory environments are also available to these children, and they experience a variety of readiness activities that relate to specific music concepts such as beat, meter, tonality, and form. Although these concepts are often presented, the teachers rarely require or expect the children to produce verbal associations for these concepts and, instead, focus on doing and experiencing.

Ideally, a laboratory should use short sessions, of fifteen to twenty minutes each, three to five times a week. Rarely, however, is such a time schedule available for either teachers or parents; weekly sessions of forty-five minutes each are workable if they are fast-paced and include a rich variety of activities and experiences. The children in the Music Experience Laboratory at the University of Arizona come once a week with their parents for a period of forty-five minutes.

THE SIZE AND SCOPE MODEL

•A music experience laboratory should include very young children.

•The ideal plan should include one session for eighteen-month-old to three-year-old children and a session for three-year-old to five-year-old children. The session for the younger children should be fast-paced and should emphasize movement. The session for the older children should emphasize imitative activities.

•Parents should be included in all activities. Up to thirty-five children may be accommodated in programs that emphasize parental participation.

•All sessions should be nonverbally oriented.

•Sessions should, ideally, be fifteen to twenty minutes in duration and meet several times per week. One forty-five-minute session per week, however, will work.

•Free time for sound exploration and experimentation should be provided for the children.

THE ORGANIZATIONAL PLAN

A music experience laboratory may be located in a place of worship, a school, a university, a community center, a YMCA or YWCA facility, or other community building. Once the location has been determined, a staff of well-trained early childhood music educators must be screened and assigned, and a well-developed publicity plan should begin. An announcement of a music experience lab program might appear in community newspapers and newsletters circulated by faculty members, organizations such as the YMCA and YWCA, and public schools. A typical press release for such an announcement includes the following information:

1. The purpose of the music experience lab program
2. The ages of the children who will be accepted into the program
3. The time and location of the lab program
4. The date of the first session
5. The cost (if any) of the program
6. The predicted outcomes of the program
7. The yearly schedule for the program
8. A list of themes and concepts that may be included in the program
9. A list of the teachers who will participate in the program
10. The date, time, and location of the preliminary meeting of parents and teachers
11. A telephone number to call for enrollment information

The Music Experience Laboratory at the University of Arizona accepts the first thirty-five children enrolled. A waiting list is maintained for those children who were not initially accepted; those on the waiting list are called when space becomes available in the program. (An attendance roster should be maintained for each lab session. If a child misses several sessions, then his or her name is dropped from the program and a child from the waiting list is invited to join the group.) Once a final list of the young participants has been determined, a letter is sent to the parents explaining the program. Such a letter should include the following information:

1. Date, time, and place of the meeting for parents
2. The location of the music experience laboratory
3. The purpose of the laboratory experience
4. A list of dates with specific themes and concepts designated for each session
5. Information about parking
6. Names of the teaching staff
7. An outline of procedures regarding the activities in the lab session
8. An explanation of the importance of parental involvement

THE ORGANIZATIONAL MODEL

•Music experience laboratory programs may be located in places of worship, schools, community centers, YWCA and YMCA facilities, or other community buildings.
•A staff of well-trained early childhood music educators should be assigned to plan and teach the program.
•An announcement of the program should appear in local newspapers, church newsletters, and in community and school newsletters and bulletins.
•A list of the children enrolled in the program should be finalized. A waiting list of children who were not accepted should be maintained, and those children should be notified of openings when available.

PREPARATION

Grouping: There are wide differences in the way children respond to music at different age levels. An eighteen-month-old child will perceive the musical activity, move at random, and will have to be guided by a parent to participate in a formal musical activity. A three-year-old will be able to respond spontaneously to the musical stimuli presented by the teacher and imitate movements and some sounds. In addition, a four-year-old will also be able to perceive and reapply some concepts and skills presented during the sessions. A five-year-old will be able to conceptualize the fundamentals of music presented through song material. This child will often respond verbally to the activities and to instructions given by the teachers. Children must, then, be placed in two groups by age level: (1) eighteen months to three years old; (2) three to five years old. Grouping by more specific age levels is even better.

The orientation meeting: In preparing for the lab sessions, one must organize a meeting between parents and teachers. This meeting should include a brief explanation of how children learn music and the musical characteristics of young children. It should also include a brief discussion of what to expect from the children who are involved in the lab sessions and what is needed to reinforce the musical aptitude development in the home environment after the lab session experience. The meeting should include an informal question-and-answer period.

Role of the aides or assistants: Aides and assistants are invaluable in a music experience laboratory program. They should be carefully instructed regarding the program goals and objectives and given specific guidelines regarding how they can assist a young child in participating in the sessions. Aides and assistants help the instructors with the distribution of sound sources and instruments and participate in lab activities such as musical games with the young children. For example, they might tap the young children during activities that emphasize a steady beat or participate in clapping games and finger plays. Aides and assistants should help the children stay in their seats and intervene in problems as they occur: Individual behavior that interferes with participation by other children in the program's activities must be changed. The atmosphere should be, however, as free and as flexible as possible in order to encourage spontaneous musical responses from the children.

Planning long-range goals: The music experiences in the laboratory are planned for the year; thus specific skills and concepts should be carefully sequenced so that their predicted outcomes achieve the program's clearly stated objectives. For example, an appropriate objective for the program could be to develop in each child the ability to audiate a steady beat (to hear in his or her mind that which is not physically present). Activities and experiences to achieve this goal should lead to each child's ability to clap or respond in some way to a steady beat.

In addition to using the conceptual framework for planning, one may assign specific themes to each lab session, so that individual sessions might revolve around such themes as the circus, puppets, Sesame Street, holidays, or animals. Each lesson is then planned using materials and activities that develop the specific theme as well as a specific skill, concept, or concept cluster.

Planning a specific lesson: Once a planning chart, listing the theme to be covered in each session and the overall goals for the program, has been completed by all of the teachers involved in the program, a sequence of activities should be developed and specific lesson plans created. The lesson plan will need to include:

1. The sequence of activities to be presented in a given session.
2. The name of the teacher who will present the activity (if more than one adult is involved in the lesson).
3. An explanation of how the activities relate to the theme and concepts being presented.
4. A list of needed materials/instruments.

An example of a typical individual lesson plan can be found in the accompanying lesson plans. This specific lesson correlates directly with an overall yearly plan of themes, concepts, and skills.

Hello, Everybody

Have the children keep a steady beat by tapping their hands on their heads, tapping their hands on the carpet, clapping their hands, and swishing their hands back and forth. Use the pop-up puppets on the macro beat (the main beat underlying the music) of the song as it is sung.

"Welcome back to the Music Experience Lab. How wonderful to have new friends in the Lab this year and to be back with you."

"We will move, sing, tell stories, and we will be very happy."

"Hello, everybody!"

Hello, Everybody!

Traditional Folk Song

Hel - lo ev-ery bod - y, yes in - deed,— Yes in-deed,—

yes in-deed.— Let's make mus - ic, yes in-deed,— Yes in-deed, my friends!

Used by permission from
G.I.A. Publications, Inc.

2. Goodbye, everybody, yes indeed,
Yes indeed, yes indeed,
Stay well and happy, yes indeed,
Yes indeed my friends.

Monkey See and Monkey Do!
(use the monkey puppet) "Our little monkey friend came back. He would like for you to do what he does. Help me!" Have the children imitate the actions of the monkey puppet as the song is sung.

Monkey See And Monkey Do

Traditional Folk Song

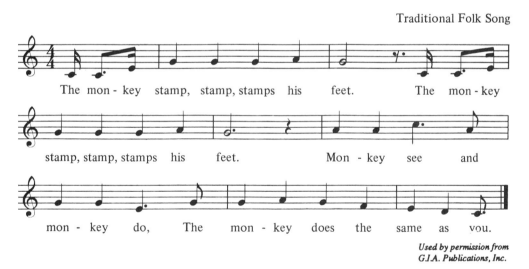

The mon - key stamp, stamp, stamps his feet. The mon - key

stamp, stamp, stamps his feet. Mon - key see and

mon - key do, The mon - key does the same as you.

Used by permission from
G.I.A. Publications, Inc.

2. The monkey clap, clap, claps his hands.
The monkey clap, clap, claps his hands.
Monkey see and monkey do,
The monkey does the same as you.

3. When you make a funny face,
The monkey makes a funny face.
Monkey see and monkey do,
The monkey does the same as you.

4. When you turn yourself around,
The monkey turns himself around.
Monkey see and monkey do,
The monkey does the same as you.

Mouse Mousie
(use the mouse puppet)
"Monkey has a friend named Mouse Mousie. She must hurry home, before the kitty chases her."
Use the mouse puppet during the song to imitate the actions. Then, provide each child with a finger puppet to use with the song as it is sung.
Repeat the song a number of times.

Mouse Mousie

Mouse mous - ie, lit - tle mous - ie. Hur - ry, hur - ry do,

Or the kit - ty in the hous - ie, Will be chas - ing you.

Used by permission from
G.I.A. Publications, Inc.

Puppet Movement
(Use the string puppet.)
Lift the hands, legs, and feet of the string puppet for the children. Have them mirror the movements made by the string puppet.
Have the children pretend that they are puppets. Have them lift their arms and legs as the pretend strings are pulled. Have the parents help the young children with the puppet movement.
Have the children continue to mirror the puppet movements as they are expanded.

Pickle Jacks
Have a finger puppet for each of the characters in the Pickle Jacks poem.
Use the finger puppets as the poem is told by:
The Old Woman
The Giant
The Smoke Elf
The Cat

There was an old woman who lived in the dell. She could catch pickle jacks out of her well, and how she could catch them nobody knew, for she never no never no never would tell!
Change voice inflections for each character.
Have the students pretend to be the characters and have them move like old women, giants, smoke elves, and cats.
Repeat this poem with the movements several times.

Ally Bally
Use a hand puppet for the song "Ally Bally."
Have the puppet sway back and forth on the macro beat of the song.
Have the children sway and move back and forth with the puppet as the song is sung.

Ally Bally

Scottish Folk Song

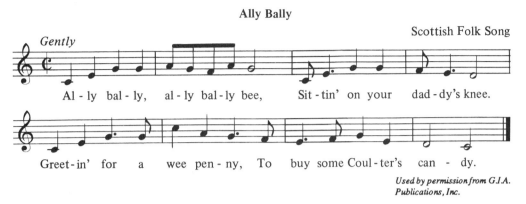

Al - ly bal - ly, al - ly bal - ly bee, Sit - tin' on your dad - dy's knee.

Greet - in' for a wee pen - ny, To buy some Coul - ter's can - dy.

Used by permission from G.I.A. Publications, Inc.

Goodbye, Everybody
Use another hand puppet in a swinging movement to the macro beat as the second verse
of "Hello Everybody" is sung to close the lab session. Have the children wave goodbye
to the macro beat of the song as it is sung.

The learning environment: A music experience laboratory should be an attractive and
colorful environment. Puppets, stuffed animals, instruments, and pictures should be displayed
throughout the room. Materials and instruments for a specific lab session should be assembled
in advance and may be placed in one area in readiness for the "large group time."

Sound exploration centers containing pictures of sound sources (such as instruments, fire
trucks, and telephones) and objects with which to create sounds should be clearly visible to the
children as they enter the lab. The objects, pictures, and toys are used to create an active
musical environment for the children and should motivate them to participate freely and
spontaneously in music making. For example, one corner of the room could have a variety of
percussion instruments made out of oatmeal boxes, coffee cans, and small margarine tubs. In
another corner there might be a variety of boxes that have rubber bands or old guitar strings
attached. Another center might have bean pods and rattles for the child to try. In addition,
guitars, drums, and barred instruments could be placed in the middle of the room. The children
should be able to experiment freely with these sound sources, but parents and teachers should
be ready to assist the children if problems occur. Uncontrolled pounding on a drum or
stamping on a guitar will certainly not produce the results needed for the young child's
establishment of a rich foundation of sound recognition.

The teacher will find it helpful to have something visual for each activity during group time.
For example, the random making of body sounds can be motivated (and controlled) by
throwing a scarf in the air and asking the children to clap, stamp, or produce sounds with their
mouths until the scarf lands on the floor; bubbles blown in the air can also serve the same
purpose, giving a visual stimulus for the production of sound. Puppets can also be used to
motivate children to imitate sounds, movements, or songs.

Identifying the children: As a child enters the Music Experience Laboratory, a name tag on a
piece of yarn is placed around his or her neck. Name tags could reflect the individual theme of
each session, after which they may be given to the child to take home. Many children collect
the name tags as reminders of the specific lab session themes. For example, jack-o-lantern
tags, made of orange construction paper with the name of the child written across each tag,
could be used for the Halloween lab session. Pictures of sound sources, such as drums or bells,
made out of construction paper, can also be effective.

THE PREPARATION MODEL

• The children in a music experience laboratory program should be grouped by age.
• Centers for sound exploration and experimentation should be provided in the laboratory environment.
• A meeting of parents should be arranged before the first session or in conjunction with the first session.
• Specific guidelines should be established for the aides and assistants in the program.
• An organizational plan should be developed, covering themes, skills, and concepts for the year.
• Specific goals, objectives, and outcomes should be identified.
• Lesson plans that relate to the goals and objectives and to the themes, skills, and concepts of the program should be developed.
• A colorful, exciting musical environment should be created for the laboratory. A variety of puppets, stuffed animals, sound sources, and other materials should be collected.
• Name tags, which are placed on a length of yarn and put around each child's neck, should be prepared.
• An attendance roster should be developed and used for each music experience laboratory.

THE LABORATORY IN ACTION

Greeting the children: As the children enter the laboratory environment they should be greeted with instruments, puppets, and sound exploratory centers. It is important to allow ten to fifteen minutes at the beginning of the session for each child to explore a variety of timbres and textures and develop his or her own vocabulary of sounds, which will be a valuable source for the later development of structured music ideas and concepts. The children may pluck the strings of a guitar or a harp, shake a variety of rattles and bean pods, and explore the sounds and combinations of sounds on barred instruments. This unorganized, free exploratory play is the informal introduction to the more structured core activities of the music experience lab session.

A specific song or chant can signal the beginning of the formal, core activities of a session. The Music Experience Laboratory sessions at the University of Arizona use the song, "Hello, Everybody" (see the first sample lesson plan for this chapter) to signal the time for structured activities and experiences. The children in the lab sit on the floor in a circle as this song is sung, and gestures and large body movements are added to the song as it is repeated a number of times.

Forming a circle: In many laboratory environments, a circle is the best seating structure for the children. In a circle formation, the children can easily see all activities, and each child has open space in front of him or her for movement activities. The concept of a circle is, however, an abstraction for the preschool age child, so specific techniques need to be employed when forming a circle of young children. The most concrete method of creating a circle of preschool-age children is to place an actual circle on the floor with paint or masking tape. A song or chant signal can then indicate that it is time to find a place to sit around this already existing circle. Carpet squares from a local carpet or furniture company can also be placed in a circle formation on the floor: The children then go to a carpet square when the signal is given for formal activities to begin.

Another technique for making a circle is to employ imagery through a song or story. For example, a teacher can invite the children to sing a song about ducks, frogs, or fish, and make the shape of a pond with their arms. Using this as a visual model, the teacher then "steps out" a pond on the floor of the classroom and asks the children to sit around the edge of the pond. (This can also be done with the image of a sun or a birthday cake.)

THE ACTION MODEL

• The beginning of the lab session should include sound exploratory activities and sound experimentation.
• A specific song or chant should signal the end of the free exploratory section of the lab and should indicate the beginning of more structured core activities.
• Guidelines for creating a circle should be established.
• Tonal and rhythmic patterns should be included at the beginning of each core activity segment of the music experience laboratory.
• Activities that categorize and organize sounds should be included. These activities could involve the use of a sound box and sound guessing games.
• A variety of movement activities should be included in every session. These activities should begin with free movement and then be sequenced into more structured, interactive experiences.
• Children should be exposed to songs that they can sing as well as songs that call for specific responses. Songs should be repeated from session to session.

THE FORMAL SESSION

Patterning: Each formal session begins with either tonal or rhythmic patterning. These repeated patterns help give syntactical meaning to the vocabulary of sound developed through the informal exploratory activities provided in the music experience laboratory. A sequential taxonomy of patterns, such as that presented by Edwin E. Gordon in his book *Learning Sequences in Music* (Gordon 1984), should be used with children on a regular basis. Following a brief period of patterning, share a variety of songs, movement activities, and sound exploratory activities with the children. In order to organize sounds and begin to categorize them verbally, large sound boxes might be constructed in the lab environment. Such boxes can be colorfully painted or covered cardboard, plastic, or wooden containers. Encourage children to bring "sounds" from their own homes to share with the other children; then place the sounds in the sound box for later exploration. Each sound is presented to the group to demonstrate the unique timbre of the sound and to demonstrate the texture created when it is played in combination with other sounds in the box. The sound box concept helps children focus on the sounds around them.

Another activity that awakens an awareness of sound and the differences between sounds is the "sound guess game." Record very familiar sounds, such as a door opening or a dog barking, on a cassette recorder, and then play the recording for the children. Ask the children to listen to the sound, out of its original context, and guess what it might be.

A sound exploratory activity can be created by constructing "sound pairs" with soft drink cans. Materials such as rice, corn, buttons, or cotton are placed inside cans, the tops of the cans are secured, and contact paper is wrapped around each can in order to make them all identical. As many as thirty cans can be filled with sound-making materials, but each should have an identical mate. Mix up the cans and ask the children to find the sound pairs. This activity helps the children to develop sensitive listening skills and creates an awareness of sound and sound sources.

Movement: Music and movement are almost synonymous for the young child. When a child hears a distinct sound or music, he or she will often respond with movement. Guided movement activities should be based initially on this spontaneous reaction to sound and music. Encourage the children to move freely in response to sounds, rhythms, and music. Eventually, these spontaneous movements can be controlled and channeled through "copy-cat" activities or attention to specific body parts. Creative rhythmic activities contribute to skill development, such as helping the child develop the audiation of beat, meter, and rhythms. These activities also help improve the child's self-concept and develop body awareness.

Imitative "mirror" activities and structured, large, body movement activities contribute to an increased awareness of spatial relationships and help to develop concentration skills. Movement games often contribute to the development of abstract thinking processes:

Beginning with self-space body movement activities, guide each child through experiences that will eventually culminate in locomotor activities involving large-group interaction, such as group sculptures (in which the children form sculptures with their bodies) and movement-tag games.

Singing: The most successful song materials for very young children are those that encourage participation and action. Simple songs with limited ranges encourage children to sing and imitate pitches. More complex song materials can be used as the child responds through movement or action. For example, the Russian folk song, "Minka," can be used to encourage body bounces and spontaneous movement activities. Because of its complexity, young children will respond to "Minka" with movement rather than song. The Scottish folk song "Ally Bally," with its limited range and soft, gentle quality, encourages singing even from the youngest children.

During a lab session, combine songs for listening with those songs that focus on participatory singing. Children should not be forced to sing: A young child who attends a lab session and just sits without singing or moving will often sing part of the song at home or will imitate a movement activity while alone. Immediate participation in singing a specific song during the lab session rarely occurs, so it is important to repeat songs from session to session.

The child's response to a series of activities in a music experience laboratory session will often be the best and most accurate factor to be considered in an evaluation of the teaching techniques employed and of the materials selected. If a child is preoccupied with running around the circle, kicking his or her shoes off, or running to the door, the songs may be too difficult or lack important movement activity required to hold the child's interest—or the pacing of the presentation may be too fast or too slow.

To be effective, individual teachers need to observe each child constantly to evaluate the child's progress or lack of progress toward beat awareness and pitch matching. If a child is having difficulty responding to the beat, make efforts to have an adult or an older child tap the shoulder or leg of the child during song and movement activities. Such external assistance will often help the child respond accurately to the beat of a song or chant. Individual patterning activities at the beginning of a lab session will also help in identifying the children who can audiate a steady beat as well as those children who are having difficulty in relating to an external beat.

Tonal patterns can assist the teacher in identifying those children who can match pitch and those who are having difficulty in audiating and matching pitches. For a program to be successful, the teachers must be aware of the individual achievement of each child in the class. These observations help in lesson planning and in establishing the instructional objectives of the program.

THE EVALUATION MODEL

•Evaluation should begin with an examination of the children's responses to the materials presented.

•Evaluation should include careful observations of individual children's responses to pitch matching and to the development of an accurate response to the steady beat of a song or chant.

•Objectives should be written in relationship to the evaluation process.

THE LABORATORY EXPERIENCE

Young children naturally respond to music—they love to move, to sing, and to make sounds. For musical aptitude development to occur, the young child needs a wide variety of musical and movement experiences. He or she needs to develop a vocabulary of sounds through free exploration and experimentation, and also needs to respond within more structured musical activities. The Music Experience Laboratory offers a unique environment for both exploratory and structured experiences in music and movement. It offers important activities and experiences in the musical arts that will help in the development of both rhythmic and tonal aptitude. The Music Experience Laboratory may be implemented in places of worship and community settings or it can emerge as a part of a collegiate music education program. It can simultaneously provide important musical opportunities for young children and a center for research and observational studies by students, instructors, and music educators.

Reference

Gordon, E.E. 1984. *Learning sequences in music*. Chicago: G. I. A. Publications.

David G. Woods is chairman of the School of Music at the University of Arizona. He is a sought-after clinician in the areas of early childhood and elementary music education. He is coauthor of music textbooks for higher education and music curriculum for Grades K–8.

The Community Education Division of the Eastman School of Music offers two levels of classes for children and their parents. The first level, for children from four months to twenty-four months of age, accommodates up to ten children in a class; the second, for two-year-olds and early threes, is built on classes of eight students. Both programs are organized in sessions that meet for fifty minutes weekly for ten weeks. Data are collected on the progress of the children with observation by graduate and undergraduate students, interviews with parents, and behavior profiles completed by the parents.

CHAPTER 2

MusicTIME and Music Times Two: The Eastman Infant-Toddler Music Programs

by Donna Brink Fox

Infants and toddlers appear to be naturally interested in music. Parents and teachers constantly observe young children's enthusiastic, spontaneous, and varied involvement with music. Haven't we all delighted in watching a youngster bounce in response to a marching band at a parade? Television commercials also capture the attention of toddlers busy at play, as the upbeat, rhythmic style of these jingles almost demands a movement in response to the sound. Infants will stop all motion and focus on the sound of a music box; older children may use songs and finger plays to reinforce ideas about numbers, letters, and colors. In fact, there seems to be no way to prevent children from displaying these musical behaviors, for during the preschool years music becomes both a means and an end—both an enjoyable way to learn about the world and a purely expressive behavior valued for its own sake.

Researchers who have studied the relationship between musical development and home environment have consistently identified the important role of parents in influencing musical behaviors at an early age (Jenkins 1976; Kirkpatrick 1962). A comprehensive investigation of successful young professionals, headed by Benjamin Bloom at the University of Chicago, concluded in its report that extremely talented people are not always born with extraordinary gifts, but they are more likely affected by the way their parents raise them and the atmosphere in their homes (Bloom 1985). Children whose parents spend time with them in making or responding to music generally demonstrate an increased interest in and aptitude for music. The relationship here is much the same as with early readers: When parents spend time reading to their children, the children develop a sense of the value of this experience.

In a similar fashion, parents become models for musical interest as they engage in musical activities with their children, taking time to play with music, demonstrating to their children a commitment to music as an important element in life and development. But how can a parent

CONTACT: *Donna Brink Fox, Eastman School of Music, 26 Gibbs Street, Rochester, NY 14604* identify and foster those musical behaviors which may appropriately be developed during the infant and toddler years? The beginning fragments of song, movement, and musical pattern that are produced by these young children hardly resemble the complicated sound and symbol system we call "music"!

The answer to this question has three crucial components: (1) It is necessary to define "musical" behavior for infants and toddlers in ways appropriate to their social, physical, and cognitive development; (2) it is necessary to provide an educational experience where parents can learn how to identify and foster these musical behaviors; and (3) it is necessary to prepare music educators who are knowledgeable in this area, so they can be responsive to this parental interest and concern.

The early childhood music program at the Eastman School of Music is an attempt to address all three of these issues. The program, based on theories of environmental influence and parental involvement in early learning, is designed to facilitate the development of adults (parents and new teachers) who can recognize musical behavior in young children and who understand how they can help it develop naturally.

PROGRAM DESIGN AND ADMINISTRATION

Community education courses for parents and children: The early childhood programs for children and parents outlined in this article are offered as classes through the Community Education Division at the Eastman School of Music in Rochester, New York. The first level of classes is called MusicTIME, for Toddler Infant Music Experience, and includes children from four months to twenty-four months of age and their parents. "Music Times Two" is the second level, which is designed for two-year-olds and early threes, again with parental participation. The maximum number of children per class for MusicTIME is ten, with eight the maximum for Music Times Two.

The classes are organized into ten-week sessions, the first in the fall and the second in the spring, corresponding to the beginning and ending dates of the Eastman academic year. The Community Education Division handles all registrations and financial aspects of the program, such as collecting fees and paying salaries. The program director for MusicTIME is a faculty member in the Music Education Department; teaching staff are recruited and trained from among graduate students and community members. Classes are approximately 50 minutes in length, and they are held at the Chester F. Carlson Metrocenter YMCA building adjacent to the Eastman School.

Early childhood methods class for preservice teachers: Both undergraduate and graduate students can enroll in a course called "Music in Early Childhood," for which a clinical experience component is assisting the teachers in the MusicTIME program. Weekly class sessions focus on awareness of expected behavior; dealing with parents in the classes; materials and resources for parents and teachers; and preparation for observation and teaching in a clinical setting.

Research in developmental music behavior: Research information on the musical development of children under the age of three years is scant, and much of it has been obtained in laboratory conditions foreign to young children. A primary research objective of the MusicTIME program is to gather data on typical behaviors in the home environment. During the final week of each session, parents are asked to comment on their children's musical behaviors at home using a form developed specifically for that purpose. This information is valuable in determining a sequence of typical behaviors, and it allows a longitudinal tracking of individual children who re-enroll. In addition, all students participating in the Music in Early Childhood course are required to write case-study reports on individual children, based on weekly observations, interviews with parents, and the behavior profiles submitted by the parents.

PHYSICAL SETTING AND MUSICAL ENVIRONMENT

Classes are held in a spacious, unfurnished room at the YMCA, with vinyl-covered foam mats available for floor seating. This room is divided with movable walls into three spaces for simultaneous group activities and sound exploration.

Sound exploration experience: Each fifty-minute class begins with individual sound exploration experiences (approximately seven to eight minutes) using sound-making toys and percussion instruments in the center room area. The children select toys or instruments from the shelving units and take them to a preferred spot in the room. Sometimes they involve another child in the play, often a parent, and after a few weeks, perhaps even a teacher will be included naturally in the activities. The majority of the play activities for MusicTIME children are solitary in nature, involving simple physical mastery of the sound: stopping, starting, hitting on the floor, hitting on the mat, and so on. Favorite toys here are music boxes and small Mexican maracas. Music Times Two children are more interested in how objects are constructed, and they are fascinated by things they can take apart or assemble. They frequently choose a toy called the "Marching Band," because it has many parts and can involve a number of people, or a "Crazy Combo," because with it they must construct their own instrument, or a small keyboard for pretend play.

Photograph by A. Sue Weisler

This sound exploration time is included because parents often regard children's playing with sound-making objects as unrelated to music. The conversations and discussions between teachers and parents during this time focus on the ways in which parents can become involved in the progression of these actions from random explorations into organizing and labeling experiences. Parents can provide support in these ways: (1) By simply *watching* a child making sounds, a parent lends value to the event through his or her attention; (2) by modeling a behavior, such as playing a drum in a new way, a parent becomes physically involved; (3) by making positive comments about the sound or action (saying, "What a great sound!"), a parent attaches verbal encouragement to the child's action; and (4) by asking questions or making statements, a parent can offer vocabulary (musical labels, such as "That was a *loud* sound!") or ideas for constructing musical patterns (by saying things like, "Let's play that again").

Group activities: In the group music session, songs are sung that can be adapted by parents using the child's name or personal items. Rhythmic chants, bouncing rhymes, and finger plays are presented for development of rhythmic skills and repertoire. Participants dance in response to popular as well as classical music excerpts. Parents remain with the group for as long as the child is cooperative; occasional trips back to the exploration space may be made to accommodate individual needs (as often as possible, these are handled by the assistants, permitting the parents to remain in the learning environment of the music group).

The primary difference between the organization of the group session for MusicTIME and for Music Times Two is in the type of material and expected responses from the children. In MusicTIME the activities are large muscle movements and whole body involvement, with parents focusing on the interaction with their own children. In many ways, the group is essentially ten dyads working side by side, with the music produced by the parents and initiated by the teacher and assistants, who provide role models for the parents. The increasing social development of the children allows the content of Music Times Two, in contrast, to become more clearly focused on individual responses and on taking turns in the music activities. In MusicTIME, a circle game might be "Ring Around the Rosy," with everyone moving and falling down together. In Music Times Two, a circle game would be "Go In and Out The Windows," with the group remaining in place and a single child moving under the raised arches.

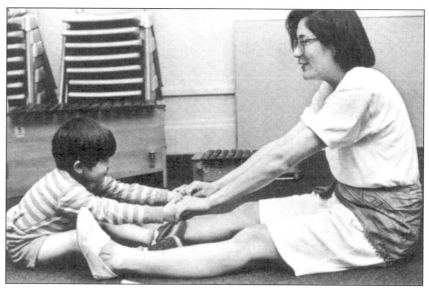

Photograph by A. Sue Weisler

EXAMPLES OF PROGRAM ACTIVITIES: MUSICTIME

In the MusicTIME classes, the parents are the primary music resources, with children involved in movements, some instruments, and initial vocalizations. Parents are encouraged to develop their musical confidence and skills in interaction with other adults in the group. Many of the activities are actually intended for use in a dyad, but they are done in a large group setting to teach the material to the parents for use in the home environment. The emphasis is on joyful participation and the expansion of repertoire for parent involvement.

Activity: Bouncing Rhymes
Description: These physical movement experiences are accompanied by rhythmic speech or chanting. For centuries, they have been part of interaction games between parents and babies in many cultures. Parents are seated either on a chair or on the floor

with legs extended, with the baby facing them (to facilitate eye contact). The baby is generally lifted with the knees on the strong pulses of the song or poem.
Example: One, two, three, baby's on my knee,

Rooster crows and away she goes!
Directions: Bounce until the line "away she goes," when you lift the baby up into the air.

Activity: Finger Plays and Toe Plays

Description: These games are focused on individual body parts, with the expectation that parents will speak or sing and touch the fingers and toes as mentioned in the text. This sensorimotor experience allows the physical sensations of touch to be incorporated into the musical play.
Example: Shoe the old horse, *(pat sole of one foot)*

Shoe the old mare, *(pat sole of other foot)*

But let the little pony run

Bare, bare, bare. *(pat soles of feet together)*

Activity: Free Movement to Music

Description: Parents are encouraged to make up their own responses to the recorded music, sometimes popular and sometimes classical. Teachers model many types of movement to help generate ideas, and people also learn from each other as they participate. The objective is to develop confidence in establishing movement responses at home.
Example: Classical: Für Elise by Beethoven
Popular: "Axel F" from *Beverly Hills Cop*

Activity: Lullabies and Quiet Songs

Description: This group of songs is intended to give parents more resources for allowing music to become a quiet part of children's daily lives, as well as for developing musical routines for relaxation and resting. Parents might accompany these with gentle, rocking motions and lots of cuddling.
Example: "Hush, Little Baby"

Activity: Action Songs and Movement Games

Description: These activities primarily use songs with movements suggested in the lyrics, such as "Put Your Finger on Your Nose." These allow children to participate in concrete responses to directions for movement.

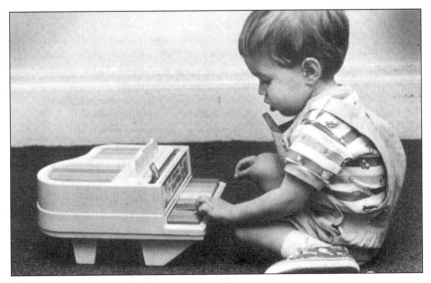

Photograph by A. Sue Weisler

EXAMPLES OF PROGRAM ACTIVITIES: MUSIC TIMES TWO

The main objective in the second level of the program is to encourage more independent musical responses from the children themselves. A secondary objective, consistent with the first MusicTIME level, is for the children to interact with other music-makers, both children and adults, in a positive and expressive atmosphere. Some children in this class spend several weeks watching before they participate during class, while others may immediately demonstrate productive musical behaviors in the group setting. Both types of activity, the "receptive" and the "expressive," are important components of developing musical skills.

Activity: Patterned Movement to Music

Description: Following the model of the teacher, children and parents use a variety of body motions with hands used together to express externally the steady pulse of the music. The motions should be done in groups of eight counts or sixteen counts so that children have ample time to observe changes in the movement and respond accordingly. The most important ideas here are repetition and sequence. The order must always be the same so that children can begin to develop their own sense of structure in the music. The music used for this activity can be varied, from classical works by composers such as Mozart to popular works like Top 40 selections or movie themes.

> *Example:* (sixteen repetitions each)
> 1. Pat the floor
> 2. Pat knees
> 3. Clap hands
> 4. Tap heads

Activity: Rhythmic Speech

Description: These rhythmic speech activities are included because they focus once again on a steady pulse, but now we add language which has a strong rhythmic pattern. Developmentally, many of these activities include large-muscle or whole-body movements. The connection to expressive language is also deliberate, as children will begin to chime in on certain repeated portions of the poems.

Example: Jelly in the bowl, jelly in the bowl, Wibble, wobble, wibble, wobble,
Jelly in the bowl.

Directions: Walk around on the "jelly line." Stop in place and wiggle side to side (or make up your own version) for the wibble wobble line.

Activity: Finger Plays

Description: Musically, finger plays are included because they help develop the idea of steady pulse and the idea of rhythm patterns. In addition, most of them can incorporate expressive use of the voice, calling for high- and low-pitched sounds, accents, and inflections. Socially, these finger plays could focus on following directions, identifying body parts, counting, or dramatizing a story.

Example: Here's the beehive, where are the bees? *(closed fist, questioning voice)*
Hidden away, where nobody sees. *(peek into hand, shake head for nobody)*
Watch and you'll see them come out of the hive, One--two--three--four--five!
BZZZZZZZ! *(uncurl fingers one at a time, fly away and "buzz" someone gently)*

EVALUATION: THE MUSICTIME BEHAVIOR PROFILE

At one of the final class meetings, parents are given a copy of the "MusicTIME Behavior Profile," which they are asked to complete during the next week and return at the final class session. The profile consists of fifty-five items of musical behavior, grouped into the categories of vocal development, movement response, exploring sounds, and participation. Each individual behavior is coded according to its frequency or consistency of occurrence at home.

In addition, parents are asked to comment on, explain, or amplify their numerical assessment by providing examples of their child's specific behaviors at home. See the accompanying figure for a portion of a completed profile for a 24-month-old boy. (The mother has no musical background other than childhood piano lessons, and the father has no musical experience or training.) The remaining fifty questions on the form appear on the following pages.

This profile of behaviors, kept on file for each child in the program, provides a longitudinal growth record for children who participate regularly. The information can also be grouped for cross-sectional comparison by age levels, for example, the records of all children ages twelve to fifteen months may be studied. In addition, the comments from the parents contribute to a rich anecdotal record of individual responses and examples of music behavior.

Musical Behavior: Participation	Score	Comments
51. Demonstrates positive interest in music experiences	3	
52. Prefers solitary music experiences. Examples *Will play instruments when left in a room alone.*	2	*Often likes to hand out instruments to company. Then conduct the group.*
53. Interested in making music with another person	3	↑
54. Recognizes familiar musical activities. Examples	3	*Time to relax & play tapes. Going to concerts. Playing piano.*
55. Requests musical activities, songs. Examples *To play his little tape player. Put the tapes on in car. Play singing games & hand movement games frequently.*	3	*When he is saying the words to songs & games alone, he does just sing but only talks.*

Example from MusicTIME behavior profile

PARENT RESOURCES

During the third, sixth, and ninth weeks of the ten-week session, parents receive copies of printed materials used in the classes, along with recommendations of resources for purchase for use in the home environment. These "Parent Pages" usually include the notation for songs used in class; texts for chants or rhymes; titles and purchase information for recordings and songbooks with suitable material; and suggestions for purchase of musical toys. The following list is a summary of the most highly recommended materials for parents in MusicTIME and Music Times Two classes:

Recordings

1. Bob McGrath and Katharine Smithrim: *The Baby Record.* Kid's Records KRL 1007 (Box 670, Station A, Toronto, Ontario, Canada M5W 1G2). Narrated by the familiar Bob from "Sesame Street" and Toronto-based music educator Smithrim, this recording contains rhymes and chants play between parent and child, as well as a section on percussion-type instruments that are easy to use with infants and toddlers. One

MusicTIME Behavior Profile

Introduction: This music behavior profile represents only a small portion of the many experiences you observe each day in interaction with your child. It is intended to describe some of the early competencies in the area of music. Remember that the Music Times Two program includes children who range in age from two years to more than three years; your child may not exhibit many of the behaviors at this point in time. The behaviors should be scored using this measurement system:

0 = not observed   1 = seldom observed   2 = frequently observed   3 = always or consistently observed

Musical Behavior Area: Vocal Development	Score	Comments
1. Coos or vocalizes when alone		
2. Coos or vocalizes in response to adult interaction		
3. Creates other vocal sound using teeth, lips, tongue		
4. Imitates parent inflection in vocalizing (rise and fall in pitch)		
5. Imitates environmental or animal sounds during play		
6. Responds correctly to directions to sing vs. speak ("can you sing?")		
7. Sings while looking at a picture book		
8. Sings to accompany other routine activity Examples:		
9. Sings along with (check all that apply) ___other children ___recordings ___parents ___other (specify)		
10. Matches pitch within narrow range		
11. Matches pitch within a wide range		
12. Creates own "songs," meandering tunes		
13. Sings fragments of existing songs Examples:		
14. Sings entire (existing) songs Examples:		
15. Sings with accompaniment ___piano ___Autoharp ___guitar ___other (specify) _____		
16. Please describe any other vocal behaviors you have observed that are not listed:		
Musical Behavior Area: Movement Response	**Score**	**Comments**
17. Turns head or moves eyes in response to music Examples:		
18. Moves arms and legs in response to music		
19. Movement stops and starts in response to music/silence		
20. Sways or rocks (back and forth or side to side)		
21. Bounces (up and down)		
22. Adds twist and turns to movement ideas		
23. Moves out into space, "dance" includes going somewhere		
24. Responds to verbal cue ("Dance to the music")		
25. Imitates dance movements ___of parent ___of television or videotape ___of another child ___other (specify)		

	Score	Comments
26. Creates own movement activities (Describe)		
27. Responds correctly to directions given in song lyrics, e.g., "Put your finger on your nose" Your examples:		
28. Plays singing games with actions at a specified time, e.g., "Ring around the Rosy: Your examples:		
29. Claps patterns of sounds, e.g., ♩♩♩𝄽		
30. Imitates rhythm patterns Your examples:		
31. Claps steady beat while singing		
32. Claps steady beat in response to recording		
33. Walks steady beat in response to recording		
34. Please describe any other movement responses you have observed that are not listed:		

Musical Behavior Area: Exploring Sounds	Score	Comments
35. Shows interest in sound-making objects and toys when sound is produced. Examples:		
36. Shows interest in sound-making objects as manipulative toys, e.g., taking the bars off the xylophone		
37. Actively makes sound with environmental objects and toys		
38. Demonstrates understanding of cause and effect; realizes that he or she is in control		
39. Shows preference for certain sound sources Examples:		
40. Uses mallet to strike individual bars on xylophone: random playing		
41. Uses mallet to strike individual bars on xylophone: imitation of adult model		
42. Plays patterns of sound on the hand drum; can repeat them		
43. Plays hand drum with both hands (flat)		
44. Plays hand drum with closed fist (drum on floor)		
45. Plays hand drum with open hand (drum on floor)		
46. Holds drum with one hand, plays with the other		
47. Plays rhythm patterns on instruments Examples:		
48. Plays steady beat to accompany own singing		
49. Plays steady beat to accompany recording		
50. Please describe other behavior in exploring sounds or playing instruments you have observed:		

Musical Behavior: Participation	Score	Comments
51. Demonstrates positive interest in music experiences		
52. Prefers solitary music experiences Examples:		
53. Interested in making music with another person		
54. Recognizes familiar musical activities Examples:		
55. Requests musical activities, songs Examples:		

MusicTIME behavior profile

advantage of this recording is the inclusion of both male and female vocal models; it is primarily unaccompanied.

2. Bob McGrath and Katharine Smithrim: *Songs and Games for Toddlers*. Kid's Records KRL 1016 (Box 670, Station A, Toronto, Ontario, Canada M5W 1G2). A production of the same duo as listed in *The Baby Record*, the activities here are more participatory, generally related well to Music Times Two content. This recording is now available as a videotape produced by Golden Books (Western Publishing); it includes Katharine Smithrim and a small group of preschool-age children in demonstration of the activities.

3. John M. Feierabend: *Music for Very Little People*. Boosey & Hawkes ISBN 0-913932-12-4. This cassette recording of a female vocalist with guitar contains material for bouncing rhymes, finger plays and toe plays, and body movements. It includes many traditional Mother Goose rhymes with British-oriented language.

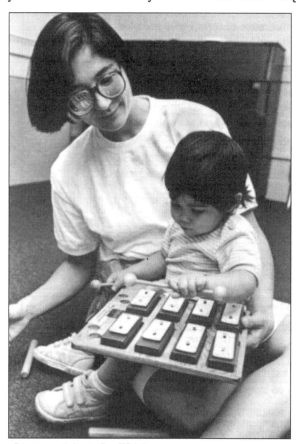

Photograph by A. Sue Weisler

Songbook Collections for Parents

1. Pamela Conn Beall and Susan Hagen Nipp: *Wee Sing* (2d ed., 1981), *Wee Sing and Play* (1981), and *Wee Sing Lullabies* (1985). Los Angeles: Price, Stern, Sloan, Publishers. These paperback books are inexpensive and available at many local bookstores. Chord and melody notation are provided, as is a cassette tape for extra guidance. Best of all, however, they fit into a purse or diaper bag for those times when we need to recall that "music hath charms to soothe..."

2. Tom Glazer: *Eye Winker, Tom Tinker, Chin Chopper: Fifty Musical Fingerplays*. New York: Doubleday & Co., 1973. This collection includes many familiar examples, with piano accompaniments and chord symbols.

Equipment and Materials

During the sound exploration segment of the class, children have access to a wide variety of commercially available musical toys and equipment. Parents have an opportunity to observe how different children play with each object. With guided comments from the teacher, they can develop a repertoire of ideas for musical play at home with sound-making objects and toys. In addition, the toys are reviewed annually to determine their potential for the class. Items may be eliminated from consideration if they are no longer available in the stores or through catalog order. A review form, listing the type and quality of sound, comments and cautions, an overall rating for each product, and the manufacturer's name and address, is distributed with the class materials handed out in the ninth session, to reinforce the concept of evaluation before purchase. (See accompanying example.)

Manufacturer Name/Address	Product Name	Type of Sound	Quality of Sound	Comments/ Cautions	Overall Rating
Toys to Grow on	Music Box	Tune	++	watch caps	****
	Jack in the Box	Tune	+	sudden action may frighten	***
P.O. Box 17 Long Beach, CA 90801	Baby's Band	Variety	--	cannot separate	*
	I Can Play a Rainbow	Octave bells	-	circular motion	*
Little Tikes	Piano	Octave "keyboard"	+	levers may be small	***
Fisher Price	Marching Band	drum cymbals harmonica tambourine maracas	++	role play, social interaction	****
620 Girard Ave. E. Aurora, NY 14052	Crazy Combo	wind	++	creative construction	****
	Piano	Octave keyboard	++	do-re-mi pop-ups	****
	Musical Activity Center	clicks, one tune	/	young infants	**
Playskool 4501 W. Augusta Blvd., Chicago, IL 60651	Musical Phone	12 pitches diatonic	elec.	battery	***
	Little Lullabye	Tune	elec.	high pitch	**
Child Guidance	Big Bird Melody Note	Tune	elec.	3 min.	*
	Musical Soft Tunes	7 tunes	elec.	pictures to assoc.	***
Peripole/ MusicPlay Brown Mills, NJ 08015	Bell Board Puzzle	C pentatonic	+	ordering skills	****
	Jingle Bells	3 jingles L-M-H	++	lollipop	***
	Musicians			role play	****

Other catalogs available from:
Childcraft Education Corporation
20 Kilmer Road
Edison Township, NJ 08817

Creative Playthings
Princeton, NJ 08540

Music materials review chart, spring 1988

TEACHER RESOURCES

Until the 1980s, most books about early childhood musical development focused primarily on children aged three years and above. The expansion of material related to early stages of musical behavior is reflected in the items below. The following references were selected for content which describes infant or toddler behaviors, along with issues related to parent involvement in early childhood programs:

Bayless, K.A., and M.E. Ramsey. 1987. *Music: A way of life for the young child* 3rd ed. Columbus, OH: Charles E. Merrill.

Boswell, J., ed. 1985. *The young child and music: Contemporary principles in child development and music education.* Reston, VA: Music Educators National Conference.

Cataldo, C. 1983. *Infant & toddler programs: A guide to very early childhood education.* Reading, MA: Addison-Wesley.

Greenberg, M. 1979. *Your children need music.* Englewood Cliffs, NJ: Prentice-Hall.

Honig, A. 1979. *Parent involvement in early childhood education* 2nd ed. Washington, DC: National Association for the Education of Young Children.

Kenney, S. 1985. "A parent/toddler music program." In J. Boswell, ed. *The young child and music: Contemporary principles in child development and music education,* 103. Reston, VA: Music Educators National Conference.

McDonald, D. 1979. *Music in our lives: The earliest years.* Washington, DC: National Association for the Education of Young Children.

Peery, C J., I. W. Peery, and T. W. Draper, eds. 1987. *Music and child development.* New York: Springer-Verlag.

Simons, G, and D. McDonald. 1988. *Musical development from birth to six.* New York: Macmillan.

References

Bloom, B. S., ed. 1985. *Developing talent in young people.* New York: Ballantine.

Jenkins, J. 1976. The relationship between maternal parents' musical experience and the musical development of two- and three-year-old girls. Doctoral diss., North Texas State University. Ann Arbor, MI: University Microfilms 77-11, 111.

Kirkpatrick, W. 1962. Relationships between the singing ability of pre-kindergarten children and their home musical environment. Doctoral diss., University of Southern California. Ann Arbor, MI: University Microfilms 62-03,736.

Montgomery, A. 1986. "Training parents in early childhood music." *Update: The Applications of Research in Music Education,* 5, no. 1, 3–5.

Wilkin, P. 1985. "A practical view of the developmental state of children's music learning." *International Journal of Music Education* 6 (November), 23–25.

Donna Brink Fox is associate professor of music education at the Eastman School of Music, Rochester, New York. Her teaching experience includes elementary and junior high school general and vocal music as well as college teaching. A founding member and current national chair of the Early Childhood Special Research Interest Group (SRIG) of the Music Educators National Conference, she is co-author of computer software for young children. The music program described in this chapter was initiated by Ms. Fox in 1985; it currently includes an additional level of classes.

The music sessions at Arizona State University, for children between the ages of twenty-four and forty months old, involve the education of the parent and child and the preparation of future teachers. Toddlers in the program explore music in a play-oriented environment; parents model music making for their children and grow in their ability to guide the child's learning through music play activities; and students enrolled in teacher-preparation courses gain methods, materials, and ideas for influencing the musical growth of the child, reporting on children's behavior, and administering early-childhood music programs.

CHAPTER 3

A Parent-Toddler Music Program

by Barbara Andress

Site: School of Music
Arizona State University, Tempe
Coordinator: Barbara Andress
Professor, Music Education

Music sessions for parents and toddlers will be offered on campus beginning April 12 and continuing for seven Wednesdays. There are openings for twelve children and their parents at these sessions, which are scheduled from 3:30 to 4:30 P.M.

The program is designed to help parents guide musical experiences for their children who are between the ages of twenty-four and forty months old. During the one-hour weekly sessions both parent and child will play with musical ideas, instruments, and objects in a specially prepared learning environment. Music specialists will be available to assist participants. Developmentally appropriate music material packets are provided each week for the child to continue the play at home. A participation fee of $35.00 will be charged for materials. For registration information call Robin Marks at 965-4374, or leave a message at the School of Music, 965-3371. Participants will be selected on a first-come, first-served basis.

The day of this news release, the phone begins to ring as parents vie to enroll their children into the limited spaces in the program. Because of the waiting list from previous semesters, relatively few openings remain.

Later, registrations are completed and the new parent-toddler music class children arrive, somewhat apprehensive, clinging to their parents, and doubtful. The warm greetings to the parent, and through the parent to the child, begin to assure the toddler that he or she can trust this experience and these strange people. Curiosity then takes over as the child enters the center to find many corners and cubbyholes full of delightful sound-making materials and to receive the assistance of new, grown-up friends in making music. With Mom or Dad tightly in tow, the toddler begins an exciting series of weekly adventures into the exploration of music.

Programs such as this require thoughtful planning, for they involve not only the education of the parent and child but also the preparation of future teachers. Research and development are a major component of these programs: Studies are devised to investigate the musical responses of children and which materials and approaches best elicit these behaviors. Understanding this network for learning involves exploring answers to the following questions:

CONTACT: Barbara Andress, Arizona State University, School of Music, Tempe, AZ 85287

•What are the philosophical basis and nature of such a parent-toddler program?
•What are its goals and objectives for the young child's musical growth? The parent's musical growth? The teacher's preparation?
•What must go on to prepare a developmentally appropriate environment for the active toddler's investigation of musical ideas?
•Who acquires or prepares the materials and guides these sessions?
•Who funds or supports the program?
•How do we know whether the experience made any difference in the lives of the participants?

MUSIC FOR THE TODDLER: A PHILOSOPHICAL STANCE

The child is the reason for the Parent-Toddler Music Program; the belief that early interaction with the joys of music can positively affect the child's life provides the program's primary justification. The overriding goal of the program is to develop within the child a disposition toward music and musical learning. This end is attained by arousing the child's curiosity about the expressive sounds of music and the many options for making them. The following nine-point credo lists beliefs that we at Arizona State University hold essential to meeting this goal:

1. *Each child will bring his or her own unique interests and abilities to the music learning environment.* Each child will take away that bit of knowledge which he or she is uniquely capable of understanding. We do not fully know how young children process and cope with information; at best, we can second-guess the process and extent of this assimilation. The child must be left, as much as possible, in control of his or her own learning. The adult's responsibility is to provide a rich environment that offers many possible routes for children to explore as they grow in awareness and curiosity about music.

2. *Children must experience only exemplary musical sounds, activities, and materials.* The child's learning time is valuable and must not be wasted on experiences with music of trite or questionable quality. Musical selections should include music of many styles and cultures; activities involve singing, moving or listening to music, and playing instruments; materials must be hands-on items such as music manipulative characters (wooden figures representing musicians and their instruments) and both orchestral and traditional classroom instruments.

3. *Children must not be encumbered with the stress of meeting performance goals.* Opportunities are available for each child to develop in-tune singing, rhythmic responses to music and instrumental awareness (playing and hearing), and to interact (listen and move) with music of his or her culture. Every child's attainment of a predetermined performance level, however, is neither essential nor appropriate.

4. *Children's play is their work.* Children learn within a playful environment. Play provides a safe place to try on the roles of others, to fantasize about powerful things, to explore new ideas, and to fit parts and pieces of things and the world together. The child's play involves imitation and improvisation; a play-oriented environment is the most effective route for this method of learning.

5. *The child evolves through several developmental stages of interactive play.* According to Parten (1930), these stages form a scale that includes play that is solitary (alone, without reference to others), parallel play (play beside rather than with others), associative play (in which association with others, not the activity, captures the interest), and cooperative play (highly organized group interaction). A parent-toddler music program must accommodate the child's ability to function within these social parameters.

6. *It is crucial that the child learn through developmentally appropriate activities and materials.* Hands-on, manipulative materials are essential learning tools. The environment and things in the environment (people and objects) are critical elements as the child engages in much self-teaching.

7. *A given learning environment will serve the developmental needs of many individual children.* Each child interacts with the material in his or her own fashion based on the child's unique gifts and the developmental stage at which he or she is functioning. A child may display sophistication and confidence in creating songs in response to dolls. Another child, in the same setting, may move the dolls around without uttering a sound—but this "silent participator" leaves the area content in having shared in the musical play. The silent participator often is later heard playing in another area softly singing to a different set of dolls—showing a delayed response.

8. *Musical modeling by parents, other adult friends, and peers is an essential element* due to the child's propensity to imitate. That which the child chooses to copy must reflect exemplary musical behavior.

9. *The parent is the child's most effective teacher,* as the bonding of love and trust is firmly established. The musically effective parent is the most powerful route to the child's successful involvement in the art. In the program, the adult friends of the toddler must work through the parent to establish their music-making bond with the young child.

GOALS AND OBJECTIVES FOR THE PROGRAM PARTICIPANTS

The parent-toddler program involves three groups of participants: the toddler, the parent or parents, and the university student from the teacher-preparation program. The objectives for each group are as follows:

The toddler explores music in a play-oriented environment, interacting with parents and music specialists; sees music making modeled by those he or she holds most dear (his or her parents) and by new adult friends; and experiences music within a free choice setting, a small group setting, and a large group setting. As a result of these interactions, the child grows in ability to perform and respond to music at a developmentally appropriate level by singing, playing instruments, exploring sound sources, moving to music, listening to music, and manipulating conceptually designed puzzles. One such puzzle might involve the manipulation of sound blocks toward the goal of matching like timbres and placing them in the puzzle board. The child's thinking skills first will be challenged to respond to the idea of music itself, and the child will then develop the ability to deal with specific music information at a beginning awareness level. For example, the child is challenged to deal with the quality of specific musical sounds by exploring the timbres of sounds, becoming aware of similarities and differences in the sounds. The child explores expressive control of sound, dealing with

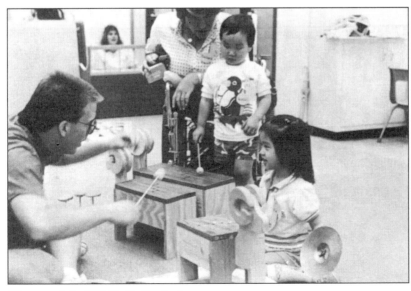

Photograph by ASU Media Production

information regarding dynamics, tempo, and articulation. The child experiences sounds that are higher or lower in pitch, and longer or shorter in duration. Same or different musical ideas are explored, leading to a beginning awareness of form. Finally, the child experiences music that represents various styles and cultures.

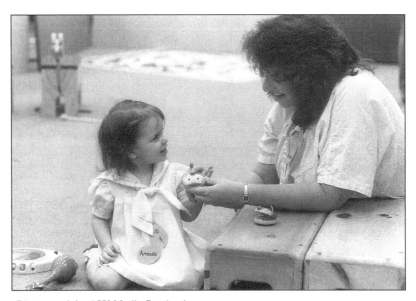

Photograph by ASU Media Production

The parent or parents participate in the program, raising their awareness level and skills as they interact with their child in various musical settings. The parents become aware of the toddler's method of learning, grow in ability to guide the child's learning through music play activities, and acquire a repertoire of song and listening materials appropriate for the child's stage of development. They acquire personal skills for simple music-making tasks, accumulate packets that are designed to promote music making in the home by the parent and toddler, and participate in an instrument-lending program where items such as Autoharps and small

Photograph by ASU Media Production

percussion instruments are available for home use on a weekly basis. Furthermore, they receive weekly newsletters that provide additional insight as to the child's expected music and play responses and participate in the program evaluation process.

The students enrolled in teacher-preparation courses are provided with methods, materials, and ideas for conducting a parent-toddler music program. The student participates by assuming various roles throughout the semester such as (1) a learner, acquiring knowledge about the development of young children and selecting or creating appropriate music materials to be used in the center, and (2) a teaching assistant in the laboratory classroom setting.

The students investigate the developmental characteristics and music behaviors of children aged twenty-four to forty months, design and prepare age-appropriate music materials for this age group, test materials in the classroom, and serve as assistants in the parent-toddler laboratory-type classroom by guiding segments of "circle-time" music play and working one-on-one in the "special interest areas." They acquire skills in working (through parents) to influence the musical growth of the child, to observe and report on the behaviors exhibited by children in the classroom setting, and to acquire and understand materials for the administration of a parent-toddler program. Optionally, graduate students may also design and implement a research study.

The first eight weeks of the semester involve the university students in learning how these young children develop and how the program is structured, and in preparing materials to be used during the sessions. Prerequisite "Music in Early Childhood" courses delve more deeply into child growth and development (from the view of child psychologists and learning theorists) than does this teacher-preparation course. This course, however, does provide an introductory look at behaviors of this age group. Among the sources of child development information used in the course is the guide to play between parents and children, *Learning Games for the First Three Years*, by Sparling and Lewis (NY: Walker and Co., 1986). This book is aimed at the practitioner's needs, using little jargon and yet communicating usable behavioral information about early stages of development. It has checklists that graphically reflect the child's development in social/emotional and intellectual/creative growth at various ages. These checklists are followed with descriptions of games that are appropriate for the age group. Though the games have not been written as music plays, the implications are clear enough that the music educator can readily transfer the games to music class. Lecture materials provide additional information as to expected behaviors of young children.

Students are responsible for preparing (1) parent newsletters, (2) weekly take-home music packets, and (3) table or area plays for the laboratory experience. Though this preparation may occur over the entire semester, much of the material needs to be completed before the children attend.

Parent Newsletters

Seven newsletters must be available for the sessions. These letters provide information as to how parents may play musically with their children and ideas for additional music activities and materials. Some of the issues of our newsletter, "You, Your Child, and Music," contain standard information; thus students are only responsible for actually writing two or three of the issues. This is often a committee responsibility.

Weekly Take-Home Packets

One of the major goals of this program is to encourage music making as a part of daily activities rather than as a special event during each week. The take-home packets provide the parent with instruments, music play manipulatives, songs, and recorded tapes to accommodate this activity. The registration fee is used almost entirely to finance the materials in the take-home packets. Due to the developmental nature of the materials, they are often constructed in-house as well as purchased from commercial vendors, making the cost factor less of a burden than it might otherwise be. The following are typical take-home packets:

Toddler song sheets: A group of song sheets or games is designed and published to

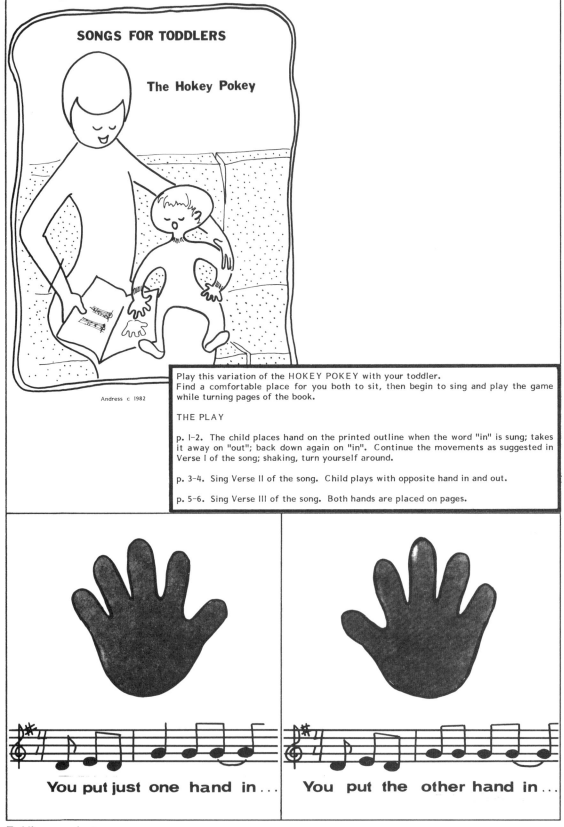

Toddler song sheet

motivate song play at home (see the accompanying example). If concrete objects are a part of the song play, those items are included.

Sound bench play: The sound bench (The World of Peripole, Inc.) is one of the more complex take-home projects. A sound bench was designed in which a small drum, two jingle bells, two maracas, and a double-headed mallet were placed. The children use the instruments to explore sounds and as accompaniments to recordings or songs. The bench can also be used as a puzzle-play game in which children remove and then replace the instruments in their proper places in the bench.

The student assistants have prepared arrangements for Orff instruments and other accompaniments for familiar songs and recorded them on a cassette tape so that the children can use the accompaniments with the sound bench. We have also recorded folk music of Mexico and an arrangement of "Jingle Bells" to challenge the children in making appropriate choices among the instruments available on the sound bench. Parents reported that children frequently carry their sound benches to the television to play along with the music on their favorite shows.

Sound bench play

Area play: At each session in the seven-week series, the toddler enters an environment where a minimum of ten music play areas are available for his or her exploration. Several of these areas (such as the "singing book place" and instrument ensemble corner) are repeated consistently throughout the sessions, but students are responsible for contributing new ideas for these activities. The students draft their ideas for area plays and show them to all members of the group, who make suggestions for refinement. After receiving this feedback, the students proceed with preparation of the plays for the children's use.

For example, one of the undergraduate students developed a plan based on the song "Hush Little Baby." A cradle, containing a soft, stuffed-stocking "baby's head," is fashioned out of a box. Several slits are cut in the top of the box, and small pictures of mockingbirds, diamond rings, a looking glass, and so forth, are attached to tongue-depressor sticks. As the child and parent or adult friend sing each verse of the song, the child places the appropriate picture stick in one of the slots.

THE SESSION BEGINS

Before any activities that involve the children, the parents attend an orientation meeting. At this time they are apprised of the program goals and of their role during the sessions. The time for activities during the one hour is explained: free-choice exploratory play (forty minutes), and large-group, circle-time music making (twenty minutes). Parents are assured of ready access to any musical assistance that may be needed while playing with their child during free-choice time. They are given a review in how to play a six-bar Autoharp, provided with a handout containing one- and two-chord children's songs, and shown some Autoharp techniques that are appropriate for toddlers.

The parents are asked to check out an instrument and use it in family music-making experiences and hands-on toddler play during the week before the children's first session. The toddler arrives for his or her first music session with instrument in hand.

The University students are responsible for preparing the learning environment for each of the parent-toddler sessions. At least one hour is required prior to the session to display music materials for the area plays and circle time experience, arrange name tags, and set out newsletters and a sheet that summarizes the session's schedule and describes the area play activities, so that parents can pick up these materials prior to the session. Parents may read the session summaries while waiting to enter the session—or afterward, as a review of the activities.

Setting up an area of play involves placing the music materials or games in an identifiable space (on a table, on a marked area of the floor, or in corners). The students prepare large posters and place them in the area for the parents' reference as to ways they might "play" in the area. For example, in the area for a "Teddy Bear Play," the poster might include pictures of the activity, suggestions for the game, a notated song, and information that it is all right if the child just plays with the figures or improvises a song about a teddy bear. The poster encourages the parent to act as a model by singing the song. Students enter the play when appropriate, adding a guitar accompaniment, singing the song, or improvising a song story about a bear.

The teddy bear activity itself is as follows: While singing the traditional song, the child turns a teddy bear figure around a central pivot, makes it touch the ground; takes the cloth and shines the shoe; and finally, on the phrase "That will do," the bear is put to bed. The child softly says, "Sh-h-h-h, nitey night Teddy Bear." The music game is played many times, as young children thrive on repetition and love to put the bear to sleep.

A Teddy Bear Place

CIRCLE TIME

After everyone has played in the special-interest areas for about thirty-five minutes, the adult friends go to each child and say, "Randy, it is almost time for circle time. I know you will want to sing and play with 'Teddy Bear' one more time, but then you will want to come and sit in the circle as we will be getting ready to sing together." This warning is important in making an effective transition from free play to the more structured activity.

During circle time a group music session is conducted. The welcome and farewell songs are always the same, as they provide a recognizable signal for activity change and closure. New songs are introduced; familiar songs such as "Old McDonald" are also sung, as they are probably already among the children's favorite songs. Repetition is very important for children in this age group, so many of the same songs are repeated throughout the sessions. We are aware that modeling is taking place for many children, and their active participation with the group is a developing skill. Often children do not seem to participate during the session, but parents tell us that they sing every song in the car on the way home.

A special feature might be introduced during a session. This might entail a performance by the college students of the themes from Prokofiev's *Peter and the Wolf* on "real" instruments as an abbreviated story is told (Peter only meets his friends, and the drama of the wolf is ignored at this stage). Children clap their hands or walk in a circle to Peter's happy melody, pausing to meet the bird, the duck, and the cat. Excerpts from the themes for each of the animals are played.

After the goodbye song culminates the circle time play, the parents and the children return their name tags, gather their take-home packets, and prepare to leave. Each packet contains a "teaching guide," and we give the parents any additional explanation they require before disbanding the group activity.

PROGRAM FUNDING AND EVALUATION

The program is self-supporting from the standpoint of take-home materials. The University provides the site, mailing costs, photocopy facilities, and other typical expenditures associated with course work. Instruments (Orff-type, Autoharps, guitars, cellos, small percussion) and other equipment are available through the resources of the Music Education Laboratory facility.

Evaluating the children: Most of the data that we use to evaluate the program reflect behavioral changes that are observable by parents and students. Students gather information through their observations of casual, incidental happenings, which they share after each weekly session. Some of the information gathered is very formal (often resulting in material for dissertations) and is collected with more formal tools, such as forms for tracking approach tendencies during the sessions and for collecting parent responses as to carryover into home environment.

One of the major activities in the center is the design and testing of hands-on materials that effectively motivate the young child to interact with music. The child is at a stage where the concrete experience of manipulating objects and sounds is a major doorway to learning. Determining what materials are developmentally usable in terms of both musical validity and the child's comprehension is an ongoing process. One of the observational tools we use (shown in the accompanying figure) helps us collect information about the child's approach tendencies, time on task, and frequency of returns. This provides data on the level of curiosity aroused in the child and the staying power of the play; information about musical interaction is scripted on the back of the form. During the parent-toddler sessions, students are assigned either to the role of teaching assistant or to that of the observer.

Parents respond with written evaluative information by completing a form that uses a four-point response scale. This questionnaire is divided into two sections: the first for parental response and the second for observed children's responses. The first section deals with the parent's comfort level and scheduling concerns. Parents are asked to indicate whether they agree strongly, agree, disagree, or disagree strongly with statements such as "The first meeting with the instructor helped me understand the nature of this program" or "The class met the goals for the children as I understood them to be."

The second section deals with the parent's perspective of his or her child's responses in both the center and in play at home. The statements rated by the parents in this section deal with the child's use of music and are rated on a scale of seldom/never, sometimes, often, and very often. Sample items from the form are as follows:

- Was excited to come to class each week
- Performed at home some of the activities used in class
- Shows more awareness of music and sounds as a result of this class
- Seemed interested in participating in activities during class (matching jingle bells, guitar, cello, bell tree, etc.)
- Used many of the ideas from class in his/her free-time play (sings own improvised songs at home; creates songs on bells at home)
- Asks parent to play with him/her in music-making activities
- Seemed to enjoy and wanted to play with the following take-home music materials: sound bench, Autoharp, wood block mouse puzzle

Observer _____

Observe all children for approximately 15 minutes, then track one or two children for remaining time.
Number of children in center _____
Age group _____ (months)
Specific individuals tracked _____   _____   _____

Description of area play(s) observed:

Observing approach tendencies
Number of children immediately interested _____

Active participants:		Nonparticipants	
Number:	**Attitude:**	**Number:**	**Attitude:**
_____	Fearful	_____	Fearful
_____	Cautious	_____	Disinterested
_____	Reluctant	_____	Distracted
_____	Watchful	_____	No space/time
_____	Aggressive		
_____	Enthusiastic		
_____	Gleeful		

Time on task/frequency of returns—tracking individuals
Child: Five-minute modules:

Child											
A											
B											
C											
D											
E											
F											
G											

Additional comments: When providing narrative information, use descriptor words (adjectives/adverbs) to reflect quality of child's response. Use back of the page for comments.

Observation sheet

In general, parental responses indicate that there is indeed an increased awareness of music and more child-initiated music making. Children and parents leave the program with great reluctance. If the most important goal of the program is to create a disposition for music, a curiosity and interest in music, then we feel satisfied that the goal is well met through the program efforts.

Evaluating the parents: Parents often enter the program willing to interact but somewhat uncertain as to how to do so. Their comfort level eases visibly as the sessions progress: During the final sessions, the parents often sing and play less—not due to their own reluctance, but because they realize that the child has grasped the idea and is able to play more independently.

Evaluating the students: The nature of the students' involvement is multifaceted. They are, however, basically evaluated on the effectiveness of their interaction with children and parents in the environment and the developmental appropriateness of the materials they produce.

In summary, a playful music-making environment for young children is essential if we are to provide a developmentally effective learning program. Play environments must contain elements of purposefulness. The possibility of musical growth, from exploratory play to some musical controls, must be inherent in each design. Through observation of young children at play, we can refine and create more effective learning materials, but in the end we must leave the child in control of his or her learning. At best, we can construct an environment rich in opportunity with many fine music-making models. If our actions are musical and honest, the child cannot help but value music as an important part of life.

Resources

Parten, M. 1930. Social participation among preschool children. *Journal of Abnormal and Social Psychology* 23, 243-269.

Sound Bench Play. Manufactured by The World of Peripole, Inc., Brown Mills, NJ 08015-0146.

Sparling, J., and I. Lewis. 1986. *Learning games for the first three years, a guide to parent/child play*. New York: Walker and Company.

Barbara Andress is professor of music education at Arizona State University, Tempe. She is coauthor of the basic music series, Holt Music K–8, *and has written articles and books on music in early childhood. She has presented sessions on music in early childhood both nationally and internationally.*

The MacPhail Center for the Arts serves children in six age groups from infancy to seven years old with the Early Childhood Arts Exploration Program. The faculty at MacPhail includes seven music teachers and a dance teacher and offers classes for children and their parents, family concerts, and music workshops. Teachers use a group-process approach to plan curricula that include listening, vocal development, the playing of small percussion instruments, and movement.

CHAPTER 4

Early Childhood Arts Exploration

by Marcelyn Smale

The Early Childhood Arts Exploration Program at MacPhail Center for the Arts seeks to encourage enjoyment of the arts throughout students' lives by developing their aesthetic perception and awareness while teaching them concepts and skills. It encourages children to interact with music at an early age in ways that are playful and creative. It seeks to provide a foundation of experiences, ideas, and vocabulary upon which they can build, whether they pursue rigorous study in music and a professional career or approach music as consumers—listening to the radio, buying recordings, and attending concerts.

The Early Childhood Arts Exploration Program includes music classes for children from infancy to second grade. There are no entrance criteria except age. Children are enrolled by their parents or guardians and attend class once a week. There, they engage in a variety of activities, including singing, movement, playing instruments, creative dramatics, and creating art projects—all activities designed to help them enjoy music and understand its basic concepts.

The classes offered include the following:

Parent-Child Participation
Music for Infants and Toddlers, ages 0–2.6
Music for the Very Young, ages 2.6–3.6
Exploring Music Together, ages 3.6–4.6
Child Participation
Musical Trolley, ages 4–5
Our Musical World, ages 5–6
(Kindergarten) Learning Music—Orff Approach, ages 6–7 (Grades 1 and 2)

Early Childhood Arts Exploration is a program of the MacPhail Center for the Arts in downtown Minneapolis, Minnesota, and serves four to five hundred children annually. MacPhail was founded in 1907 and offered graduate and undergraduate degrees as MacPhail School of Music for many years. MacPhail Center is now a department of the Continuing Education and Extension of the University of Minnesota. It is a member of the National Guild of Community Schools of the Arts and a nondegree-granting institutional member of the National Association of Schools of Music. Approximately three thousand students study at

CONTACT: Director, Early Childhood Arts Exploration, MacPhail Center for the Arts, 1128 LaSalle Avenue, Minneapolis, MN 55403

MacPhail each year, most of them receiving private or small group studio instruction from MacPhail's ninety-member faculty.

MacPhail's early childhood faculty currently includes seven music teachers as well as a dance teacher who is responsible for creative dance offerings. Teaching loads for the music teachers range from three to ten classes per quarter, depending on enrollment, seniority, and scheduling considerations. Minimum qualifications for teaching in the program include a bachelor's degree in music, music education, or early childhood, and experience teaching music to young children. At present, the staff includes two teachers with doctorates and two with master's degrees. Nearly all of the teachers have completed additional study in Orff-Schulwerk, Kodály, Dalcroze Eurhythmics, or Education Through Music. Staff turnover has been minimal; the most senior instructor has been teaching in the program for seventeen years.

Each class in which parents are not present includes an assistant who helps with preparation of materials, serves as teacher's aide, and provides the safeguard of having a second adult present in case of emergencies. Many assistants are preschool teachers; others are music education or music therapy students. Assistants are paid for the hours they work; most perceive the job as informal student teaching or in-service experience that offers the chance to work closely with a master teacher. Assistants in the program have provided a pool of candidates for new teaching positions, and all teachers hired are required to assist in another teacher's class for their first year.

Each classroom in which early childhood music classes are taught is equipped with a piano, a tape player, a variety of small percussion instruments, a rug or carpet for sitting on, and plenty of room for movement. Other materials and equipment used in the program include two to three full sets of orchestral instruments and assorted folk instruments, a library of picture books, songbooks, early childhood music textbooks, recordings of classical and children's music, and a wide variety of art media (from construction paper to stickers to plastic cups to tempera paints) for use in class projects.

The students in the early childhood program come from all socioeconomic levels, but the majority come from upper-middle-class families. They come from all over the Twin Cities (Minneapolis–St. Paul) metropolitan area and from outlying communities.

Frequently, preschool children come to early childhood music classes while their older siblings, alumni of the program, take instrumental lessons.

The early childhood music program makes a concerted effort to reach and educate parents as well as children. This is done through parent-and-child classes, through parent workshops, and through printed lesson summaries that children receive at every class. Firmly believing that parents can be the most effective music teachers and models for their children, the program's instructors offer parents handouts filled with information about children's musical development; lists of books, compositions, and other available resources; and descriptions of techniques that they might use to help their children progress. Parents are urged to visit their child's class once each quarter; this often increases their ability to communicate with their children about the lessons.

Once each quarter, a family concert is offered. This "happening" is designed to be developmentally appropriate for children ages three through eight, and it is closely tied to the Musical Trolley curriculum, which focuses on the families of instruments. At each fifty-minute concert, a professional ensemble such as a percussion or string quartet or a woodwind quintet performs. The narrator, one of the early childhood teachers, encourages children to listen for musical elements they have learned about in class. The children respond by tapping the steady beat, by circling their arms during legato passages, by changing their motions for the B section of an ABA piece, and so forth. Active participation is made easy at these concerts by encouraging the audience to bring pillows and sit on the floor. A favorite part of each concert is a story, arranged by a local composer, in which audience, instrumentalists, and narrator each take the part of different characters. In "The Gingerbread Boy," for instance, the viola demonstrates the movements of the old woman as she makes the cookie; the audience sings and the violin plays the song of the gingerbread boy; the bass takes the part of the bear who tries to catch him; and the cello is the silky-voiced fox.

To increase the program's visibility in the early childhood community and to perform a

A happenings concert. Photograph by Peter Berglund

service for that community, the early childhood teachers frequently offer music workshops for local and state early childhood organizations. Whenever possible, they also allow interested teachers to observe classes. They serve as resource people in their specialty and are often called upon for information and advice.

HISTORY OF THE PROGRAM

In 1968 a new class for preschool children was offered at MacPhail Center. It was called the Musical Trolley and offered children experiences with music and puppetry (and, at first, a snack of milk and cookies). Soon after the beginning of the program, the administrators of MacPhail and the University of Minnesota Continuing Education and Extension channeled resources into the program and hired a teacher/administrator and two more teachers. A precedent was set that remains a major strength of the program—the teachers planned each lesson together. (This group-process approach to curriculum planning was later adopted for the planning of a second-year offering that expands the children's repertoire to include the music of other cultures (Our Musical World) and for refining courses that were originally designed and taught by individuals.) Although individual teaching styles differed, the teachers all taught the same basic lesson, shared ideas that worked well, and discussed how to improve the lesson for the following year. They developed a team approach to all aspects of the program, sharing responsibility for preparing the art materials and typing the lesson summaries.

The curriculum was also expanded to include Musical Trolley Express, which filled the needs of children who wanted to take Musical Trolley but were too old for the regular classes, and Orff Music for Children, serving first and second grade children. A Dalcroze class was offered, and a class in creative dance was added.

The first parent-and-child class was begun in 1979. It served children 2½ to 3 years of age. Unlike established classes, which followed a sequence of lessons spanning three academic quarters, Music for the Very Young was designed to be a single-quarter class of eleven weekly, sixty-minute sessions. The course content had the double purpose of introducing children to musical ideas and instruments and teaching parents techniques for continuing their children's music learning. Because of the popularity of this course, two other parent-and-child courses were added, each with five sessions. Music for Infants and Toddlers welcomed families with new babies as well as the two-year-olds. Exploring Music Together brought a music class to children who were almost, but not quite, old enough for Musical Trolley (4–5 years old).

The program has also expanded to other locations: Musical Trolley and Music for the Very Young classes are now offered in St. Paul and at suburban sites, where parking is free and access is easy. In addition, MacPhail now contracts with other organizations to offer classes at their locations, including nursery schools, day-care centers, community centers, and a sports and health club. The program has also responded to changes in the needs of families by expanding offerings in the late afternoon, the evening, and on Saturday.

Financial support from the University of Minnesota has been very important to MacPhail Center: In 1988, approximately 25 percent of MacPhail's $2 million budget came from the University. The rest of the revenue for the Center came directly from student tuition and fees. Each student in the Early Childhood Arts Exploration Program paid eighty dollars for eleven weeks of 1½-hour Musical Trolley classes. Teachers earned $500 for teaching that class, and assistants earned $440. The cost of outfitting a single site with the necessary equipment for teaching Musical Trolley (classroom percussion, tape player and recordings, art supplies, miscellaneous materials, and key orchestral instruments) is approximately six thousand dollars. Careful planning has allowed sharing of equipment between sites, but the expansion of the program to multiple sites was possible only with special grants.

THE CURRICULUM

Music for Infants and Toddlers: The five hour-long sessions of this class, for families with children under 2½ years of age, provide models of musical interaction for parents and children. The primary source of material for this class is the rich heritage of American folk songs and singing games. Folk songs are used to greet children, to stimulate their language development, and to promote physical activity. The folk songs chosen are repetitive and easy to learn and lend themselves to variation and improvisation. Two book-and-cassette sets recommended to participants in the class are: *Heartsongs* by Leon Thurman and Anna Peter Langness (1986), and *Music for Very Little People* by John Fierabend and G. Kramer (1986).

The class has a secondary focus on vocal development. Each week, the teacher models vocal exploration activities; parents try the activities themselves and encourage their children to imitate them in vocal exploration. Equally important, parents learn to imitate their children's vocal play in order to reinforce their vocal development.

A typical class begins with the teacher singing a greeting song ("Hello, Matthew, do-oh, do-oh, I'm so glad you're here") to each child, using the tune "Shake Those Simmons Down." Next, the song "Here We Go 'Round the Mulberry Bush" offers toddlers opportunities to move in many ways, with locomotor and nonlocomotor actions. Infants participate while held in their parent's arms, receiving aural and kinesthetic stimuli. A finger play or pat-a-cake activity

The Greeting Song

Tune: American Folk

Hel - lo Mat-thew do oh, do oh, Hel - lo Mat-thew do oh, do oh,

Hel - lo Mat-thew do oh, do oh, I'm so glad you're here.

focuses the child's attention onto the sequence of actions called for in the rhyme. Then comes another action song, "Skip to My Lou," sung (in this example) to the words "Round and round we go." Everyone makes circles with fingers, hands, or feet, then turns around in a circle. Before the song ends, the toddlers are moving around and around the room.

Next, the children play small percussion instruments. For example, tambourines are used when the theme of the class is circles. A soothing, recorded orchestral selection follows to calm the group. Over a five-week period, parents and children are introduced to works ranging from a movement from one of J. S. Bach's Brandenburg concertos to a selection from *The Carnival of the Animals* by Camille Saint-Säens. After the listening selection, the children and parents work together on a visual reminder of the theme for that week's class. In response to the circle theme, they might draw big and small circles on large sheets of paper. The class then sings about their pictures, using still another folk song such as "round and round, old Joe Clark, round and round I say...."

After the class reviews songs and singing games from former sessions, the teacher sings to the tune of "Shake Those Simmons Down" again, this time singing "good-bye" to each child. Some of the children are reluctant to leave, but the ritual of the song seems to help. A number of parents use the melody for greetings and good-byes and sing the song when those occasions arise at home.

Music for the Very Young: Like the class for infants and toddlers, this class is designed to introduce parents to techniques for helping their children learn about music. Many parents, however, have expressed their appreciation of this class as a first experience with group learning activities for their child. Children who cling to their parents as they begin the class soon walk happily to the other side of the room to put their instruments away on the shelf or sit down by the teacher to read a book. The teacher frequently becomes very important in the lives of these children and parents are often asked, "Is today music day?"

Three organizing principles are considered when planning each class session. First, each

Cello in Music for the Very Young. Photograph by Peter Berglund

session includes ritual and repetition. Every class begins and ends the same way: The children can count on performing their favorite songs and finger plays every week.

The second consideration is to provide children with the opportunity to explore instrumental timbres. The "instruments of the day" are grouped according to the way in which they are played: those that are shaken, tapped (woodblocks, drums, or triangles), rubbed, strummed (harp or Autoharp), blown (woodwind), and those that are buzzed (brass).

The third organizing principle involves a progression each week from group activities, which are largely teacher-directed, to free-choice play in learning centers. In these centers, children are free to explore and review the instruments of the day, make puppets to take home, play the piano, or read books.

The accompanying Music for the Very Young handout lists the new activities included in a typical class. (It does not include the review activities, which often take a third of the class time.)

Music for the Very Young—Session 5

Lesson focus: Today we will focus on instruments we rub.

Song: We will sing a Swedish folksong, "Ritch Ratch," accompanying it with two different sounds of the rhythm sticks and with body percussion.

Instruments: Today we play bumpy instruments—those with a grooved surface, like rhythm sticks and *guiros*, and those with a raised surface, like sandpaper blocks. The sound varies with the surface, of course, but it also varies with the rubbing implement. Try rubbing a *guiro* with a rhythm stick, with the *guiro*'s own stick, with your fingernails. One of the most satisfying at-home instruments for rubbing is a grater, but use a carrot rather than your fingers for rubbing!
   We will always feel the vibrations that are produced when we rub a fluted rhythm stick. Sound is *always* produced by vibrations, whether by a violin bow rubbing a string, a mallet hitting a drum, or fingernails scraping a blackboard.

Game: We will use sandpaper blocks to imitate the sound of a train while we chant:

Engine, Engine, Number 9,
Going down Chicago Line.
If the train goes off the track
Will I get my money back?

We will also make a "movement train" and go for a ride.

Listening: We will listen to an orchestral work by Sergei Prokofiev called "Departure." It depicts a train ride, starting out slowly, then speeding up, and finally slowing down again as it reaches its destination.
We will listen for the sound of the sandpaper blocks in Leroy Anderson's "Sandpaper Ballet."

Story: We will read a book by Marcelyn Smale about "Wanda the Worm" and her very special, sandpapery nose.

Art: We will make a touch book so that we can tell the story of Wanda the Worm at home. We will also make our own sandpaper blocks using polystyrene.

Music for the Very Young handout

EXPLORING MUSIC TOGETHER

In this five-session course, the goal is to promote the children's formation of beginning concepts associated with each element of music, to increase facility in the basic skills of singing and beat competency, to strengthen music-listening skills, and to increase enjoyment of music. The course's goal regarding the parents is to provide increased knowledge of how children develop these skills and concepts and to model techniques by which parents can help children learn. The course also seeks to provide a repertoire of songs and singing games appropriate for preschool children, opportunities for parent and child to share in pleasurable music-making activities, and materials to promote sharing of songs or music at home. The course is organized so that one element of music is emphasized each week—timbre, rhythm and duration, pitch, dynamics, or form. It is designed to be especially appealing to families that cannot afford the time or costs of a longer course.
   A typical class begins with a fingerplay/chant, then a song to welcome each parent-child duo. The session that emphasizes the element of form continues with simple stop-and-go games, played by the children and parents. These games begin with the players responding to the

teacher's cues. Each child then takes his or her turn as the leader for the group, showing by simple hand motions whether the others should play instruments or be silent. Another time, the lesson is extended with the teacher playing an instrument as the class moves to the sound or stops when the instrument stops. Each parent-child duo then gets an instrument and plays the game, one of them moving and the other playing the instrument.

After learning a chant such as "Charlie over the Ocean," metallophones and glockenspiels are introduced, and children are encouraged to accompany the chant with "water sounds" on the instruments. They explore ways to move as boats. Then parent-child teams decide on a way to put together some of the different things they have done with the chant, using voices, instruments, and movement. Each team performs its version (its form) for the group.

A listening lesson completes the session. The teacher tells a story in which the pattern of interactions between characters matches the form of the Brahms *Hungarian Dance No. 3* in F. The class listens to the music, identifies the themes, and makes stick puppets of the characters and acts out the story while listening to the music. Finally, the chant that began the class is repeated as a closing activity.

MUSICAL TROLLEY

The most obvious organizing factor for the Musical Trolley curriculum is the focus on families of instruments. In Musical Trolley, children explore nearly every instrument of the orchestra over the three-quarter (thirty-three week) sequence, along with many folk

Baritone horn in Musical Trolley. Photograph by Peter Berglund

instruments. During the fall quarter, they play percussion; in the winter quarter, they play strings; and in the spring quarter, they play wind instruments. The instruments used are owned by the early childhood program.

Children learn to produce tones on each instrument. They compare instruments and discover reasons for different timbres. Children do not become proficient on an instrument; they just get acquainted. The value of this introduction becomes obvious when children notice and recognize instruments on the sound tracks of television shows, when they decide they want to learn to play an instrument, and when they express confidence that they will be successful at it.

Individual sessions each have a focus, such as piano/forte, steady beat, ABA form, high/low, rondo, or vocal exploration. This focus is carried throughout the lesson so that children experience concepts aurally, visually, and kinesthetically. Each session includes a new song, a listening activity, a book or story (usually dramatized), activities with classroom percussion, a game or other eurhythmic activity, a new instrument, and an art project. Sessions are 1½ hours long, except for the late afternoon and evening classes, which are shortened fifteen minutes. Class size is limited to twelve or fifteen students, depending upon the size of the classroom.

The accompanying Musical Trolley handout outlines the principal activities in a typical lesson. Every session contains review activities and time for children to interact with each other and with classroom materials. The handout itself is important to most Musical Trolley students; many families make a booklet of the lessons and pictures of instruments.

Saxophone in Musical Trolley. Photograph by Peter Berglund

OUR MUSICAL WORLD AND ORFF MUSIC FOR CHILDREN

These two classes are designed for school-age children. Our Musical World is for kindergarten children who have already taken Musical Trolley. It expands children's repertoire of American folk song and adds an introduction to the customs, folklore, music, and instruments of other cultures. Children increase their knowledge of classical music, adding opera and electronic music. They begin reading rhythmic notation.

The MacPhail Center has been built upon the vision of a few administrators, the dedication of many teachers, and the excitement of thousands of children and their parents. It continues to flourish because it provides teaching of high quality, using methods that allow children to interact actively with real instruments and music of aesthetic quality.

Musical Trolley—Week 3

Lesson focus: This week we will focus on crescendo (gradually getting louder) and decrescendo (gradually getting softer) in music and movement.

Songs: We will review "I Had a Cat" (from last week), remembering some of the animals we included in that song. Our new song is "The Farmer in the Dell." As we sing and play a game with our new song, we will add a person each time we sing a new verse. Then, when everyone has been added, we will lose a person each time!

Instrument: The saxophone is our new instrument this week. We will learn that this instrument is a member of the woodwind family, even though it is made completely of metal. We will compare the saxophone reed to the clarinet reed. We will also locate the bell, keys, mouthpiece, and neck on this instrument.

Listening: We will hear the saxophone featured in a jazz selection, "Toy," by Julian ("Cannonball") Adderly. We will hear the crescendo as each instrument is added. We will also listen to "In the Hall of the Mountain King" from *Peer Gynt* by Edvard Grieg. We will dramatize this story about Peer's adventures in the Hall of the Mountain King, showing how the music gets louder and louder, building a huge crescendo.

Game: We will stretch elastic bands as we hear a crescendo and let them get smaller as the music gets quieter. Then we will try the same thing with a rubber band large enough for us to all get inside.

Eurhythmics: We will find ways to show a crescendo with our bodies as we hear crescendos played on a hand drum or on the piano.

Instrument playing: We will make crescendos and decrescendos with classroom percussion instruments and learn to identify the musical symbols for crescendo and decrescendo.

Literature: We will discover a visual crescendo in the book *Where is Everybody?* by Remy Charlip (1957). As the story develops, things are added one by one. When it begins to rain, things are lost one by one until nothing is left.

Art: We will create a classroom mural from the story of Peer Gynt, placing all our illustrations within a huge crescendo symbol.

Taking music home: Try singing your favorite songs, varying the dynamics so that you gradually get louder or gradually get softer. Listen for the crescendos made by sirens as they approach (and the decrescendos as they go away).

Musical Trolley handout.

References

Charlip, R. 1957. *Where is everybody?* New York: William R. Scott.

Fierabend, J., and G. Kramer. 1986. *Music for very little people.* Farmingdale, NY: Boosey & Hawkes.

Thurman, L., and A. P. Langness. 1986. *Heartsongs.* Englewood, CO: Music Study Services (P.O. Box 4665, Englewood, CO 80155).

Marcelyn Smale is a member of the music education faculty at California State University, Chico. Before this appointment, Ms. Smale taught early childhood music for nine years at MacPhail Center for the Arts in Minneapolis, serving as administrator for the Early Childhood Arts Exploration Program for four years.

Using an eclectic approach, Music for Children encourages the development of self-esteem through musical expression, creative and divergent thinking, and the development of musical and listening skills. The program seeks to make connections between music and the life experiences of the young child.

CHAPTER 5

Music for Children

by Mary Ann Hall

illustrations by Catherine Minor

Music for Children is a child-centered program dedicated to the development of self-esteem through musical expression. Based on the idea that the primary instrument in early childhood music education is the child, Music for Children provides the physical and psychological space for children to make, do, and internalize music and, as a result, to grow to feel "I am the music—I am partner with the music."

The program is eclectic in approach, drawing principles and some experiences from Kodály, Dalcroze, Orff, Pace, and others. Learning is approached as an exciting, pleasurable process that encourages growth through planned and spontaneous expression. In addition to encouraging the development of self-esteem through musical expression, Music for Children experiences encourage creative and divergent thinking through music, the development of musical and listening skills, and instrumental exploration (including hands-on experience with over thirty instruments). Guided by teachers, children explore rhythm and melody, harmony and form, and dynamics and tempo through singing, dancing, instrumental exploration, dramatic play, eurhythmics, and active listening.

BUILDING SELF-ESTEEM THROUGH MUSICAL EXPRESSION

The most important goal of Music for Children is that every child feel affirmed through music. Because we place such importance on building self-esteem, a large part of our preparation time is spent on "affirmation-presentation." We eliminate judgment and competition and focus on affirmation and cooperation. Feeling affirmed, young children are eager to participate musically, free to create musically, open to share musically, and happy with their own musical contributions.

The system of affirmation-presentation allows children, in a very short time, to feel safe to share ("Listen to my song"), feel free to share ("I found a way to play"), and feel assured that their contribution will be accepted (one initially shy four-year-old told the teacher, "I wanna dance for everybody. Play the music and watch me dance").

Welcome: A class begins. Eight to twelve children arrive. We are present, both physically and emotionally, to welcome the children. We press a button to start the opening music and, with music playing, go to the door to welcome the children. We might say, "I'm so glad you're here. When you get your socks and shoes off, join me at the rug. The music is playing just for you," or "Hi, Susan. Hi, Brett. Hear that music? We call it jazz and it's playing for you. When you're all set, we'll dance to that jazz."

CONTACT: Mary Ann Hall, MFC, P.O. Box 3457, Sawgatuck Station, Westport, CT 06880

During every class, we sing about each child. We know that a child's name is one of his or her most important possessions, so we sing or speak each child's name in a song, a rhyme, a chant, or a rhythm pattern. We always sing each child's name in a "hello" song:

Hello Song

Traditional

Hel - lo Lind - say Too-da - la, __ Too-da - la, __ Too-da - la. __

Hel - lo Lind - say Too-da - la, __ Too - da - la my friend.

Using a puppet with a movable mouth, we sing a portion of the song to each child, having each child feel the rhythm pattern through the puppet on an arm, a finger, or a knee.

We often sing each child's name in other songs that beg to be personalized:

Mary Wore a Red Dress

Traditional

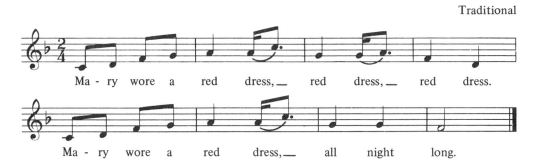

Ma - ry wore a red dress, __ red dress, __ red dress.

Ma - ry wore a red dress, __ all night long.

We always use each child's name as part of a rhythmic or melodic response game. For example, after the opening music, we gather in a circle on the rug and sit down for a change of pace, a song or two, and a name response game. The name response game varies according to the developmental age of the group. It could start with the teacher simply saying the child's name and the child echoing the teacher, and it could develop into something much more complicated as the children grow musically, physically, and intellectually. Some more complex examples might include the use of melodic patterns associated with the child's first and last names, played out with a combination of body sounds (such as hand claps, knee slaps, and toe taps), and the notational matching of these sounds.

We always sing about children who are present, but we also sing about children who are absent. Every child knows that we care about him or her, and that we sing about them even if they are not present. When a child who has been absent returns, we are present with, "I'm so glad you're back." Parents hear this message and know that their child was missed, that their child is an important part of the class, and that we value their child's presence. Parents need affirmation, too.

Singing about things from home: When the children arrive, any treasures they may have brought from home are placed in a basket in the middle of our rug. After the opening music activities, in which we use the child's name in a song, rhyme, or chant, we sing about these possessions, responding to the child's precious offerings from home. Each possession gets a little song, and is then put away until after class. A truck may get the song:

Roll That Truck Around and Around

Source unknown

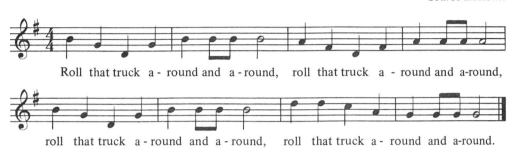

Roll that truck a - round and a - round, roll that truck a - round and a-round,

roll that truck a - round and a - round, roll that truck a - round and a-round.

A teddy bear may get the song, "Teddy bear, Teddy bear, turn around...." If we don't know a song that fits an individual child's treasure, we make one up. We feel very strongly that these extensions of play and home need to be acknowledged. This recognition takes only a few minutes, and it's a wonderful musical experience for these children.

Making affirmation statements throughout class: Throughout each class, we make affirmation statements that encourage participation and build the child's positive feeling of self. We have found that the words we choose to use are as important as the experiences we choose to share. The style and language of the presentation is as important as any other aspect of our music program. Some examples of "affirmation statements" are: "Susan found a soft way to play," "Daniel sang way up high—Let's all do it," and "You found a way."

Throughout each class we also sing songs that accomplish these same ends. An example of an "affirmation song" for the very young child is:

Emily Play Your Sound

Mary Ann Hall

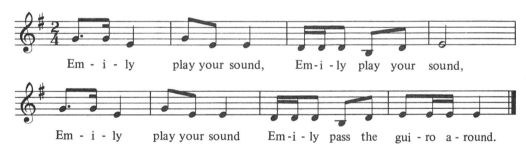

Em - i - ly play your sound, Em-i - ly play your sound,

Em - i - ly play your sound Em-i - ly pass the gui - ro a - round.

Celebration: We end each class with a celebration. This celebration is complete with songs, rhythms, and a natural snack. This has become an important tradition for all of us at Music for Children. There is something special about coming together to share a song and a snack. The magic of the moment encourages participation—sometimes even solo singing—from the shyest child.

Apples and Bananas

Source Unknown

I like to eat, eat, eat, eat. I like to eat

ap - ples and ba - na - nas. __ I like to eat, eat, eat, eat.

I like to eat ap - ples and ba - na - nas. ____

Good-bye: As each child leaves, we sing good-bye. As with the hellos, we often sing our good-byes with a puppet.

At this time, we also give the children a "sneak preview" of what's coming next week. We might say, "Next week we're going to play a story on the piano. Don't forget your fingers." There is a link between feeling good and performing well, not only in music but in all areas of learning and of life. Music is a powerful tool for building positive feelings of self, feelings that we early childhood educators can support, for now and for later.

Goodnight Ladies

Traditional

Good - bye John - ny, we'll see you next week. *Can't wait!*

MAKING CONNECTIONS

In addition to our emphasis on building self-esteem through musical expression, one of our most important beliefs is that music must connect to the life experiences of the young child. When a child feels that music is a part of all that he or she does, that child has begun to build a powerful and positive relationship with music that will last a lifetime.

We want children to feel and understand that music is a part of the world they live in. After all, whales sing, the thunder roars, birds chirp, and the wind howls. Rocks and shells make great instruments. We collect seashells and tree shells and sing:

Seashell, Oh Seashell, Oh Where Did You Come From

Mary Ann Hall

Young children should understand that music is a part of their living experience and not just a subject to be taught. After all, mommies and daddies croon lullabies to their babies; there's music at our celebrations, parades, weddings, birthdays, and festivals; movies, television, and radio all use music to create moods and add an aesthetic dimension that enhances the medium and captures the audience; books and poetry are full of the rhythm of words and the inflections of melody; and concerts and special music programs are an important part of our community life.

We connect music to feelings, literature, art, nature, family, play, natural food, celebrations, reading, mathematics, and so forth. Our connections often begin with a book. For example, we have used *The Pea Patch* by Thatcher Hurd (1980) after dancing to our opening music for the day, Dan Emmets' "The Pea Patch Jig." The book captivated the children; they were literally swept off their feet to dance the music again. We have also used *The Snowy Day*, by Ezra Jack Keats (1962). As we turn the pages, we sing what we see in the pictures, using the traditional melody, "What Shall We Do on a Winter's Day?" Some of our favorite verses are "Let's make tracks on a snowy day"; "Let's smack a tree on a snowy day"; and "Run in the snow on a snowy day." We ended the session with a eurhythmic experience inspired by the last page of the book: "Walk with a friend (mom) on a snowy day; Run with a friend on a snowy day."

What Shall We Do On A Winter's Day

Traditional

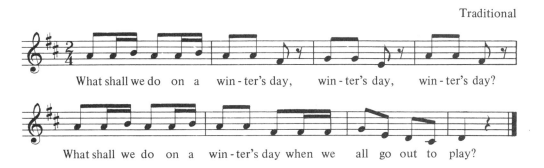

The child as instrument: In our atmosphere of affirmation and encouragement, children grow to feel that they can dance, sing, move, create, and play music in specific ways on specific instruments. We encourage them to sing, to the tune "Ten Little Indians":

> I can make music with my hands
> I can make music with my hands
> I can make music with my hands
> I can make music, yes I can!

I can make music with my feet
I can make music with my voice
I can make music with my whole body
I can make music, yes I can!

I can sing the music: At every level from age two to age eight, singing is an essential element of our program. From September through May, each child, at each level of development, sings and acts more than one hundred songs, extending and developing the child's natural affinity for singing. We experiment and create with our voices. We sing individually and as a group, and we sing and play our own accompaniments on a variety of instruments. We sing our own songs and traditional songs, we sing songs from musical comedy, we sing classical songs, and we sing popular music.

I can dance the music: Many times, we act on the music as we sing. We dance it, move to it, add dramatic play, add instrumental accompaniments, add sound effects, or connect the music to a book, a story, a poem, a painting, or an artwork.

We always start with opening music. As the children enter our learning environment, the music is playing, inviting the children to "come be my partner." Our opening music varies each week and introduces our children to an infinite variety of musical styles and musical possibilities. Because we believe that young children need time to be free with the music before being asked to be specific with it, we dance a combination of free dance and directed dance, and we move with a combination of free movement and directed movement.

An invitation to listen and dance might sound like this: "Music is powerful. It can spin you around or jump you up and down. It can dance you around or help you clown around. It can soothe you to sleep or put the beat in your feet. Listen! The music will tell you what to do."

Arthur Getz's *Humphrey the Dancing Pig* (Getz 1980) encourages dancing. In this book, Humphrey decides that he wants to be slim like the cat, and he begins to dance. We prerecord selections that fit Humphrey's dances: Native American music, rock and roll music, ballet music, and whirling dervish music. As each dance comes up in the book, we play the appropriate music and dance, returning at the end of each selection to discover what comes next. This is a marvelously fun way to introduce children to various styles of music and dance.

Oh, Great Spirit

Yuma Indian Song

Oh,— Great Spir - it, Corn— is dy - ing,

Oh, - Great Spir - it, Corn— is dy - ing, Ah - wah.____

(whisper)

Ah-wah.____ Ah-wah.____ Ah-wah.____ Hi

"Oh Great Spirit," a Yuma Indian chant, creates a sense of concern and a sense of celebration.

I can move to the music: Jacques-Dalcroze connected music notation and fundamental movement. We feel that this connection is one of the most important contributions to music education. We continually develop eurhythmic experiences that give children the opportunity to internalize rhythms, to "physicalize" rhythms, and to have a kinesthetic awareness and understanding of music. These eurhythmic experiences are also designed to capture, engage, and enchant the young children who we teach.

"Rabbit Run on the Frozen Ground" is one of our favorite songs. Coupled with our eurhythmic game, which includes a tease and tag between the children and the teacher, this song definitely captures, engages, and enchants. We talk about footprints, the possible, and the impossible. We sing the song, and after the children are a bit familiar with the tune and the words, the game begins.

Rabbit Run

Traditional

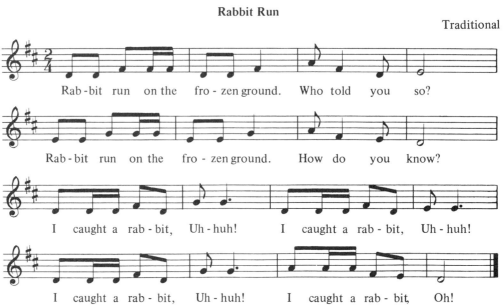

Rab-bit run on the fro-zen ground. Who told you so?

Rab-bit run on the fro-zen ground. How do you know?

I caught a rab-bit, Uh-huh! I caught a rab-bit, Uh-huh!

I caught a rab-bit, Uh-huh! I caught a rab-bit, Oh!

The teacher strums a rhythm on the guitar, and the children run to the rhythm they hear. As they run, the teacher sings the first phrase, a question. The children respond by singing the second phrase, and the running and the conversational singing continue through the third and fourth phrases of the song. When we arrive at the fifth phrase, "I caught a rabbit, uh-huh," the teacher reaches out to tag the children who are running on the frozen ground, pretending to be rabbits. This game is designed to protect the rabbits; the teacher cannot move from a sitting position, so being caught is up to each child. If tagged, the rabbits are fed pretend carrots and given a pat on the head and a few loving remarks and we begin again, this time with another rhythm. For example, the rabbit need not only run on the frozen ground, but may also walk, skip, slow, or rest.

These experiences with this wonderful folk song lead the children to internalize and understand rhythm. The response between the teacher and the children reinforces the children's feeling for and understanding of musical phrasing, and the tease and tag part of the song game helps make all of this an irresistible musical experience.

CREATING AND PERFORMING

I can create the music: We are continually tossing out invitations to create. Sometimes the invitation to create, to invent, is spoken: "Sing your own song"; "Play your own rhythm"; or "Create your own dance." Sometimes the invitation is part of a song or a poem, as in the following song that encourages free expression on a melodic percussion instrument:

Play the Marimba Two by Two

Mary Ann Hall

Su - san and Jon - a - than two by two.

Play the ma - rim - ba just for you.

I hear the music: Active listening is connected to every aspect of our music program. We create listening games that extend and develop a child's awareness of the highs and lows, the fasts and slows, the louds and softs, and of the repeats or contrasts of sound in music. One example of a listening game that we play with our three-year-old children during the parent/child part of the class is a frolicking, staccato piece that is combined with a smooth and gently flowing lullaby. A story, such as *Jump, Frog, Jump* by Robert Kalan (1981), sets the scene:

We invite the children to come close for a story. The children respond by chanting "jump, frog, jump" at just the right time to get the frog away from some impending danger. When the book is read, we set the scene—asking the children to pretend that they are the baby frogs, and asking the parents to pretend that they are the mommy and daddy frogs.

We give the children the following instructions: "When you hear the jumping music (which we illustrate with an example of staccato music), jump! When you hear the sleeping music (which we illustrate with a lullaby), sleep. Find your mommy or daddy and snuggle in his or her lap. Take a pretend nap, but keep listening in your sleep. You never know when I'm going to play the "jump, frog, jump" music again. Listen—the music will tell you what to do." The children respond with great enthusiasm (and so do the parents); the children hear, act on what they hear, and show by their actions that they understand what they hear.

We believe, as did Zoltán Kodály, that each of us is born with a sense of rhythm, a sense of melody, and inner hearing (the ability to hear or reproduce sounds inside the mind when no sound is physically present). We help young children to become aware of this ability for inner hearing, and we share many experiences at all the levels that extend and develop this natural ability.

For example, in the familiar song "Little Cabin in the Woods," the motions substitute for the sound, phrase by phrase, until the children sing the entire song inside their heads as they make motions that represent the words. The children also sing the letters listed in the song "Bingo" inside their heads. They sit, outwardly silent, and listen to the letters inside their heads and then join in singing out the last phrase, "And Bingo was his name-o."

We also clap the rhythm patterns of songs the children know very well, and encourage them to match a tune sung inside their heads with the rhythm pattern of the "mystery song" they hear on the outside. We sometimes use even more complex experiences, including singing alternate phrases inside the head and aloud and singing entire songs inside the head.

I understand the music: The children's responses say it all: "I hear a walk rhythm." "I hear even rhythm." "I hear a trombone." "That music is moving up high." "I hear a man's voice." "I can play a story on the piano." "That's an accelerando."

I can read the music: As with all other aspects of our program, we approach music reading creatively. The children begin to read because their experiences, acting directly on music and internalizing the music, lead them to read the music: Every music experience contributes to understanding, which contributes to music literacy.

Some techniques we incorporate into this effort to plan experiences that lead directly to music reading are: eurhythmic experiences that connect fundamental movement to musical movement and notation (representing walking with quarter notes, running with eighth notes, skipping with dotted rhythms, and so forth); rhythmic experiences that connect sound patterns to rhythm patterns; rhythmic experiences that connect sound patterns to notated rhythm patterns; melodic experiences that connect melodic movement to physical movement; melodic experiences that connect melodic movement to Kodály hand signals; and melodic experiences that transfer melodic movement to recorder, to piano, or to pitched percussion instruments.

I can write music: Writing music begins very early. As soon as the children begin to see music, they begin a process that leads them, when they are developmentally ready, to write music. At first, the writing is an extension of their play, their art, and their stories. Later, the writing becomes connected to specific sounds that the children hear in their heads and from other sources.

I can play music: We introduce specific studies on recorder and piano to children ages six, seven, and eight. Our approach to the instruments is child-centered, creative, and makes connections as often as possible. For example: A South American story about a turtle who plays the recorder to get himself out of trouble introduces the children to their first recorder song—a three-note song (using the notes *b, a,* and *g*) that is created by the child. Each child has the power to tell the story with the recorder to friends and family, punctuating the story with their own recorder melody.

Children who learn through this child-centered music program have had hundreds of experiences acting on melody, rhythm, harmony, and form. More important than all the skills developed, however, is the fact that the child has a genuine love for music and a contagious excitement about music. We believe this happens when one understands the young child and music, and can be that special teacher who creates the magic to make such a program come alive.

References

Getz, A. 1980. *Humphrey the dancing pig*. New York: Dial.

Hall, B. 1973. *Harry the hippo and friends*. Westport, CT: Music for Children.

Hall, M. A. 1982. *Take a bite of music, it's yummy*. Westport, CT: New England Association for the Education of Young Children.

Hall, M. A., and D. Eastman. 1988. *Piano play*. Westport, CT: Music for Children.

Hall, M. A., and P. Hale. 1982. *Capture them with magic. It's music, it's dramatic play, it's excitement in learning*. Rowayton, CT: New Plays Books.

Hall, M. A., and B. Hall. 1987. *Snug-a-love songs* (book and tape). Westport, CT: Music for Chilldren.

Hurd, T. 1988. *The Pea patch*. New York: Crown Publishers.

Julliard Repertory Library. 1970. Cincinnati: Canyon Press.

Kalan, R. 1981. *Jump, frog, jump*. New York: Greenwillow Books.

Keats, E. J. 1962. *The Snowy day*. New York: Viking.

Mary Ann Hall is the founder and director of the Music for Children program. She has taught at all age levels, and currently works both with young children and as an adjunct professor at Bank Street College, New York City. She is a consultant, a contributing member of the editorial board of First Teacher, *a song collector, a songwriter, a performer, and a prolific producer of materials for young children.*

The New Age School, a nonprofit organization, gives students thirty minutes of music instruction each day, and music-making activities are used throughout the curriculum. All areas of learning are integrated to provide a creative educational experience. Children at the school are between the ages of 2 ¹/₂ and 9 years old, and are taught in classes of eight to twelve students.

CHAPTER 6

Placing the Arts at the Core of the Curriculum

by Diane Cummings Persellin

T wo young women had a dream. They visualized a child-centered preschool that would integrate all areas of learning into a lively, innovative curriculum. The arts from many cultures around the world would be at the center of the curriculum. This preschool would be a place where the unique imagination and skills of each child would be lovingly stimulated and enhanced. It would be a warm and caring environment where children would be given the opportunity to develop skills in creative thinking and artistic expression.

In 1965, this dream became a reality. Isabeth Hardy and Belle Graubard purchased a large, old brick house in San Antonio, Texas, and opened the New Age School. Established initially as a preschool, the New Age School has grown from five students to more than seventy children now ranging in age from two and one-half to nine years old.

The philosophy of the school is based on an understanding of child development as described by Jean Piaget and as witnessed in the creative learning process by early childhood educator Maria Montessori, composer and music educator Carl Orff, and artist and humanitarian Nicholas Roerich. The children are encouraged to experience the world imaginatively, creatively, and cognitively. There are definite expectations within parameters, but children are free within those parameters.

The director of the school, Judith Wade, explains that children have a sense of reality that often differs from that of adults. Children are not necessarily always in training for adulthood; they relate to the world from their own perspective while enjoying the act of learning at their own pace. There are only two rules at the school: Act toward each other in a respectful way, and respect school property and the property of others. Children are given many opportunities to learn these rules together. It is the hope of the school that this will be translated to actions outside of the school as well.

THE SCHOOL SETTING

The New Age School is housed in a residential neighborhood and bordered by a large playground to the east and a small city park to the west. In front of the building is a flower garden that is planted by the children with brightly decorated placards with the pictures and names of the flowers there. Behind the brick house stands a carriage house that has been converted into two comfortable classrooms. An office has also been added recently.

Each room has been brightly painted. The music room, which once served as the living room

CONTACT: *Judith Wade, Director, or Anita Narramore, Music Teacher, New Age School, 217 Pershing, San Antonio, TX 78212* of the house, is a large area in which "morning circle time" takes place with all seventy children and eight teachers. It is carpeted, and a large blue circle on the carpet has been created with masking tape to help the children sit or stand in a circle.

Only the music instruments that are to be used on any one day are on display; the remainder are stored in a large cupboard. A piano, a stereo, and a guitar are available to the music teacher. Bookshelves line the walls of the hallways, and child-created mobiles of the solar system are found in classrooms. Block-printed quilts greet the guests at the front door, and large works of art painted by children, parents, and local professionals are found throughout the house on the walls. The responsibility taken by each child in creating much of the school's decor exemplifies the active learning approach stressed by the school.

FUNDING AND ORGANIZATION

The New Age School is a private, nonsectarian, nonprofit institution, licensed by the Texas Department of Human Resources. It is funded by a combination of tuition, grants, and private donations. Tuition is kept as low as possible to allow children from families of all income brackets to attend the school. Rather than turning away children because of lack of funding, a barter system has been developed: In exchange for tuition, parents offer their services as carpenters, plumbers, and teachers.

Fund-raising events are also held to defray the costs of the school. Parents, teachers, and board members hold arts and crafts shows and cake sales on the porch of the school to raise money for needed equipment. The director of the school keeps busy writing applications for grants to cover tuition and renovation projects.

Classes range in size from eight (for the youngest children) to twelve (for the older students). The teachers frequently divide these classes in half to give children more individualized attention. Occasionally, teachers combine classes of different age levels to encourage children to share and to learn through other children. These mixed-age classes are called "sister classes."

The preschool runs from 8:30 A.M. until 2:30 P.M. with extended hours available from 7:00 A.M. until 6:00 P.M. Three part-time teachers assist with the after-school program, which has an average enrollment of about forty children. Last year this program included physical education, creative dramatics, dance, music, and art and was sometimes centered around the Saxon epic *Beowulf*. Children were told the story, acted out the parts, created simple costumes and scenery, and improvised an instrumental accompaniment for the drama.

Although the emphasis is on process rather than product, parents are sometimes invited to attend a performance that the children have created during regular school hours or during the after-school program. These informal sharing times usually involve the kindergarten and older children, but sometimes include the younger children as well. The preschool children may present these creations on their own, or they may be assisted by some of the older children. They especially enjoy creating their own dances, based on stories or on a field trip, to an accompaniment provided by the older children.

THE TEACHERS AND THE GENERAL CURRICULUM

The eight teachers at the New Age School all hold bachelor's degrees, and some hold advanced degrees. Each teacher has charge of a homeroom of eight to twelve children; they often exchange classes so that students may benefit from their various areas of expertise. These areas of specialization include music, art, language arts, science, mathematics, French, Spanish, and physical education. Cooking classes are also popular with the kindergarten, especially when children get to sing about what they are making and eating.

Because all teachers work with all children, a strong sense of community pervades the school. The weekly staff meetings often include a song or poem created by a three-year-old in music class or an art project created by a five-year-old. Parents regularly share songs with the music teacher; they also perform on musical instruments for the children. Professional teachers, parents, and children work together to teach each other and themselves.

All areas of learning are integrated in order to provide a creative educational experience. An overall theme for the school is selected each week. This theme may be a country, a concept from science, a myth, a legend, an epic, or a story from folk literature. The theme is carried out through all of the classes during that week. The song from the morning circle time may be repeated in the music classes, but it usually serves as a jumping-off point. Rhythmic and melodic chants from the morning circle song may be created, or new activities based upon the theme may be introduced. The circle often serves as a sharing session for some of the more creative products from the week.

For example, a typical week's study unit might begin with the telling of the French folktale "Puss in Boots," followed by a French folk song during the morning circle time. The next day the children may then retell the story in their own words and dramatize it, first speaking the parts of each character and later singing the parts. The children may create a simple repeated pattern on Orff instruments to accompany their "opera." To provide a more complex accompaniment, the five- and six-year-olds may play while the three-year-olds sing. The children may continue with work on several French folk songs and may create their own songs and dances about cats.

In science, they may study the cat family; in math, they may count the cat's toenails (five in front and four in back). In language arts, they learn the hard sound c in the word *cat*. In art, they may use watercolors to portray the story of "Puss in Boots" or model their own cat in clay.

A traditional theme at the beginning of each year is a story called "Star Babies." In retelling the story, it takes on an almost magical quality as the three-year-olds fantasize about when they lived on the stars. They create a star music dance and accompany each other on the Orff instruments, often with some guidance from an older child. This dance becomes more elaborate in the music classes as new instruments are added to the texture. An informal sharing of this dance may take place on Friday at the morning circle time.

THE MUSIC CLASSES

Children at the New Age School have music classes, taught by a specialist, every day for thirty minutes. Sometimes the youngest students are divided into two groups, each meeting for fifteen minutes, to allow for more individualization. The teacher plans lessons that help the children to imagine, create, and express their own music.

A music experience may be set up in stations: Four to six children rotate through four stations. Each station requires minimal assistance from a teacher: One might consist of an activity such as experimenting on a tonebar instrument while the teacher asks some questions about the sounds that the child is making. Another station may involve singing into a PCV piping held from the child's mouth to his or her ear to enable the child to hear his or her own singing voice. A rhythm instrument, placed in a circle made with masking tape, makes a popular station. Children also enjoy discovering chiffon scarves at a station and moving with these scarves—especially when the teacher plays the recorder.

In a typical thirty-minute music class, a minimum of six or seven activities is planned for the children. There is not a heavy emphasis upon acquiring a large repertoire of songs for these young children: The goal is that of making the child responsible for producing his or her own music, and giving the child a better self-image as his or her musical ideas are valued and developed. Children do this by exploring sound sources, acting out short stories and poems, accompanying their stories with instruments, creating their own words and music based on the story of the week, and moving to improvised or recorded music. (This recorded music is usually ethnic music from other countries, collected by the teachers or shared by parents; it may also be solo guitar or piano music.)

For example, a teacher may ask the children to retell the story from the morning circle time. The teacher then chooses four statements about the story, suggested by the children, and creates a short, rhythmic chant. When all the children know this chant, individual students are asked to offer melodies for each line. This is done line by line, and the teacher repeats each line, singing it much as the child has suggested. Through the teacher's guidance, children learn about phrases that ask questions and about those that give answers. She briefly notates this new song and then teaches it to the entire class. The children then discuss which tonebar instrument would be the most appropriate for the mood of this particular song. Several instruments may be explored before the class reaches a consensus on the best one. This process may take half of the class period, and this new song may be performed for the school at a later morning circle time. Imagine the thrill the children must receive at having their composition performed for the entire student body.

Children enjoy classifying the sounds of the instruments by categories such as woods, metals, drums, and sticks. The teacher labels the categories for the children and later asks leading questions such as, "Is this a high sound?" or "Can you play a soft sound?" In this way, children acquire a music vocabulary.

Children are encouraged to move expressively to music as well as to learn to keep a steady beat. Expressive movement is encouraged by moving with scarves and ribbons or acting out a part of a magical story. The older elementary children who have grown up through this program are very comfortable with movement and dramatic play.

Finding and developing the child's singing voice is a crucial first step on the road to musical independence. The teachers use finger puppets to help children find their singing voices by singing a question to the child via the finger puppet. The child will respond via his or her puppet, often losing any self-consciousness in an effort to help the finger puppet respond to the questions. Children also enjoy singing "yoo-hoo" calls and responses and making siren sounds to help them find their singing voices.

When teaching a new song to the children, the teacher will often sing one line of the song and ask the children to sing an echo. The teacher is careful not to sing with the children when they are echoing, but models correct singing and lets the children sing on their own so they can hear their own voices. Because these young children have music class every day and are encouraged to find and use their singing voices, pitch-matching is not a significant problem by the time they leave the kindergarten class.

MUSIC BEYOND THE MUSIC CLASS

Informal music instruction, allowing children as many opportunities to express themselves through music as possible, often begins or takes place in all of the classrooms—not just in music class. The classroom teachers are encouraged to use music as much as possible in their teaching but are not required to have any special music background. The director of the school is interested in black spirituals and shares her record collection and her love of this music with the children. One of the teachers is an opera enthusiast and enjoys sharing parts of his favorite operas with the children. The faculty's new German teacher is eager to share German folk songs with the children. The creative and supportive atmosphere encourages the teachers and children alike to express themselves freely.

Often, informal music instruction will also take place on the playground or in the small park that adjoins the school. All of the children, from the youngest to the oldest, play on the playground together: The music specialist is on the playground with them and takes ideas from their play—accompanying them on the recorder or guitar. For example, she may stand next to the playhouse with her guitar, strumming softly. She may borrow a playground chant that is sung by one of the children as he or she jumps from the playhouse, and echo and embellish that chant. She may later build on these ideas during the music class.

Sister classes often take field trips with each other and share musical experiences together. The three-year-olds may go to the zoo with the seven-year-olds. The older children help the younger children see over the railing at the zoo and later act out the parts of different animals when back in school. The older ones help the younger children decide what kind of instrumental accompaniment would best suggest each animal during the zoo dance.

Musical examples are drawn from classical and folk music so that children may see how their music fits into the broader musical spectrum. Children are also introduced to a large variety of folk instruments such as a dulcimer or guitarrón. A Vietnamese mother taught the children several of her native folk songs and then shared a tape of Vietnamese opera with the children. Children initially laughed at the different tone quality of the voices, but came to appreciate the beauty of this different style of vocal production.

Children respond enthusiastically to the performers who are frequent guests at the school, either during the morning circle time or later in the day. In the past, these performers have ranged from a large semi-professional choir from Minnesota to many parents and other solo performers. The music teacher is an accomplished recorder player and enjoys performing for the children in class and on the playground.

The New Age School is a dedicated approach to integrating the arts in the curriculum—a direction that should lead to a greater appreciation of the fine arts in later life. With teachers, parents, and children pulling together to create and share the beauty of the arts, the experience cannot help but reveal and foster the beauty in every child.

Diane Cummings Persellin is associate professor and coordinator of music education at Trinity University in San Antonio, Texas. Her many workshops (both in this country and in Australia), together with her publications, deal with her interests in early childhood music and with learning and teaching modality strengths.

The state of Texas mandates and funds prekindergarten education for students with limited English proficiency or with economically disadvantaged family backgrounds. Music teachers in the Austin Independent School District use approaches that include the traditional full-class learning environment and learning centers to work with large classes of preschool children, giving them experiences with singing concepts and skills, music listening, and responses to music through listening and playing.

CHAPTER 7

More than Music: Two Approaches to Teaching

by Mollie Tower, Holly Davis, and Susan Carden Parker

Since the early part of this decade, the state of Texas has targeted education reform above all issues. Among the reforms generated by the legislature in 1983 was the emerging recognition of the importance of early childhood education for high-risk students. In a special session during the summer of 1984, the legislature passed House Bill 72, mandating prekindergarten education for high-risk four-year-olds in Texas schools.

This bill enacted far-reaching measures for early childhood education, intended to break the debilitating and costly cycle of remediation, school failure in the later grades, and the dropout problem by building a solid foundation for school success. This type of action is supported by long-range studies, which clearly document the value of early education programs. These studies show that young adults who attend high-quality preschool programs demonstrated greater gains in education, employment, and social responsibility than did similar young adults who did not attend.

Prekindergarten education in Texas is mandated and funded for students whose Limited English Proficiency (LEP) or economically disadvantaged family background might impede their success in school and in life. The program stresses intensive language development in a curriculum divided into five areas: communication development, cognition development, motor development, fine arts, and social and emotional development.

Music specialists in Austin deal specifically with the elements categorized under Music and under Theater Arts. The "Music essential elements" are singing concepts and skills; music listening; and responses to music through listening and playing. The "Theater Arts essential elements" are expressive use of the body and voice and creative drama.

TEACHING ENGLISH AS A SECOND LANGUAGE

Much of the teacher's work falls into the English as a Second Language (ESL) category. Teachers develop the student's English by activities such as speaking slowly and acting out simple statements to associate word meaning with body movement. For example, the teacher can act out sentences such as "I can play the drum," and then have students act out similar sentences. Teachers also use visual materials, including picture cards, wall charts, and books, for reinforcement. They concentrate on activities that sharpen the senses (particularly seeing and hearing) to aid in the development of reading readiness skills. They use short sentences

CONTACT: Mollie Tower, Elementary Music Coordinator, 6100 Guadalupe, Austin, TX 78752

and simple words in story telling, and introduce words for familiar objects such as food, clothing, parts of the body, and other objects found on field trips or in the classroom.

The beginning of the school year can be difficult for teachers who are not bilingual. Students whose proficiency in English is limited are often timid. Teachers who have a minimal vocabulary in Spanish and Vietnamese seem to be able to ease this transition time, and as the year progresses, the LEP students acquire more English vocabulary and participate more actively and comfortably. The disadvantaged youngsters must also acquire vocabulary for academic success: Although all of the students come to school with language, it is not the language necessary for success in school. One of the greatest contributions the music program can make to this group of children is to expand children's vocabulary and the images in their minds' eyes.

In the Austin Independent School District, music specialists currently serve seventy-one classrooms, each of which has twelve to fourteen students. Classes, which are often combined with physical education classes for a typical class size of twenty-four students, meet for a forty-five-minute period, two or three times a week. The first time most of our music specialists taught prekindergarten students was in September 1987. There was limited time for special training or curriculum development, so we held a series of in-service sharing sessions during the 87–88 school year to help ease the great concerns most music specialists had about dealing with four-year-old students. Two outstanding music specialists, Susan Carden Parker and Holly Davis, had especially great success in the first year of this special program. Holly Davis drew upon her background as a kindergarten teacher and set up her music program reflecting concerns for an "exploratory plan" approach to learning, an approach that involves the preparation and use of interest centers. The "full class" approach presented by Susan Carden Parker provides helpful information about setting the stage for learning when dealing with a large group of very young children for a lengthy time span.

FOCUS ON THE FULL CLASS
by Susan Carden Parker

The approach to music education for the prekindergarten child that I favor is to maintain the traditional full-class teaching environment in which the children remain in a large group, doing the same tasks for the entire class time (forty-five minutes). Since this is a long period of time to hold the attention of a four-year-old child, the activities must be continually varied and group management techniques must be maximized.

MANAGEMENT

To work successfully with a large class of prekindergarten children, one must establish clear parameters for each move they make. I make this structure evident from the minute the children enter the music classroom. The individual's space in the room is defined, and each child is expected to find his or her place independently. Ideally, there should be some kind of marking on the floor or carpet that the child can easily identify as his or her own place to sit. In a situation where this is not possible, the edge of the carpet, a length of clothesline, or a piece of masking tape placed on the floor can define where an individual student should sit. All movement is then directed to and from the child's individual place.

Signaling is a helpful tool for maintaining order in my prekindergarten music classes. Since music is an aural art form, aural cues are highly appropriate. One example of an aural signal is ringing a bell and having the children put up "quiet signs" (one finger raised in front of closed mouth). Clapping is another good aural cue that does not require any extra equipment. For instance, establish a routine of clapping three times, having the students clap in reply three times, then keep their mouths quiet and place their hands in their laps. When engaging in movement activities, let the music become the signal to begin and end the experience. The children remain seated until the music begins and sit down where they are when the music ends.

To help children understand the signals, I carefully explain and model what the signal will be and what the children should do in response. I then give the signal, asking a few students to show the desired behavior while I praise their quick responses. By presenting the signal, modeling the desired behavior as a game, and lavishly praising the children who respond correctly, I usually have the entire class responding to the new signal by the end of one class.

Careful planning of transition times can eliminate many of the problems that often arise when dealing with this age-group. As a general rule, seated children behave in a more orderly fashion than standing children, primarily because their potential for moving and causing problems is limited. Let the class sit in their places while only a few children at a time move when changing places, selecting partners, choosing instruments, or joining a circle. This allows the teacher to monitor the student's behaviors carefully. When a child who is setting a good example is chosen to move first, the other children will all try to match the example of acceptable behavior. If a child is chosen to move and cannot follow directions, he or she must wait for another chance to try.

I include a full range of activities from calm to very active. These activities are used to implement the prekindergarten music curriculum, which emphasizes the basic controls or elements of music: intensity, duration, pitch, and timbre. Each of these elements must be experienced and understood before any other musical knowledge can be developed. When introducing intensity, the most basic concepts are loud and quiet; for duration, the concepts are fast and slow and steady beat; for pitch, high and low; and for timbre, the classification of sound sets. Introducing these concepts at the beginning of the school year and incorporating them into each lesson helps me establish a common vocabulary with the children. A balanced curriculum for prekindergarten children should be taught through singing, playing instruments, listening, and movement.

SINGING

Through songs, the prekindergarten child develops both singing skills and language skills. At the beginning of the year, when both of these skills are relatively undeveloped, I am faced with the difficult challenge of selecting appropriate songs. This is especially true when working with Limited English Proficiency (LEP) students. I begin with songs that are very repetitive, with only a few words changing in each verse. The slight change is enough to keep the children from becoming bored with the song and to enable them to master the rest of the words. One example is the melody of "Skip to My Lou" with new words "hop, hop, hop in a

Students seated in their own places

circle" (repeated three times), "hop in a circle now": The direction to hop may be alternated with words such as walk, tip-toe, jump, or fly.

Using "piggyback" songs (songs that have words that go with traditional melodies such as "Skip to My Lou," "Mary Had a Little Lamb," or "Twinkle, Twinkle, Little Star") also helps to maximize participation during singing. These songs are very easy for children to learn, and words can usually be found to fit a variety of topics. Careful planning and thoughtful song selection by the teacher will provide opportunities for even the most language-deficient child to participate and to succeed.

Children like songs with nonsense syllables and actions. Any catchy melody can be given neutral syllables such as "la," "pop," or "dum" (an all-time favorite). With different body movements for each verse, the song can continue until the teacher is ready to drop. Songs with animal sounds are very useful because the teacher can sing the song with children responding only with the appropriate animal sounds. A favorite song for my students is "I'm Bringing Home a Baby Bumble Bee" from Reilly and Olson's *It's Time for Music* (Van Nuys, CA: Alfred, 1985), used in the accompanying lesson plan.

Sample lesson plan
Grade: PK

Materials:
Resonator bells (C and F; four pairs)
Tape recorder
Tape: "Flight of the Bumblebee" by Nicolay Rimsky-Korsakov.
Books: Barton, Byron. 1973. *Buzz, Buzz, Buzz.* New York: Macmillan; Reilly and Olson. 1985. *It's Time for Music.* Sherman Oaks, CA: Alfred.
Icon Charts showing bumblebees

Singing	Moving	Listening	Playing
✓	✓	✓	✓

Anticipatory set and warm-up activity: Students stand. Teacher throws yarn ball and makes different "buzz" sounds (high and low). Student echoes sound when throwing ball back.

Objective and lesson focus: In this lesson, the student will play the pattern C C F ("bumblebee") on the melody bells. Focus-pitch.

Instructional input:
1. Teach the song "I'm Bringing Home a Baby Bumblebee" with motions. Emphasize "bumblebee" (C C F). (From Reilly and Olson 16–17).
2. Show bumblebee icons, choose correct pictures, demonstrate pattern on bells; have children play the pattern on the bells in groups of four.
3. Listen to "Flight of the Bumblebee" to show bee movement. (boys—green carpet, girls—brown carpet).
4. Read the book, *Buzz, Buzz, Buzz.*
5. Have the students line up and learn the beehive chant:
Here are the beehives, (*make fist*)
Where are the bees?
Hidden away where nobody sees.
Soon they will come creeping out of the hive. One, two, three, four, five. (*open fingers*) Buzzzzzzzz (*fly away*)

Assessment: Each student performs the simple melodic pattern on the bells as part of a group of four students. Class signals when the pattern is played correctly.

PLAYING INSTRUMENTS

The music teacher has a veritable treasure in the classroom rhythm instrument set. There is very little a prekindergarten child will not do to "get to play" an instrument. Playing instruments is an activity that works very well with LEP students because few language skills are required and much of the behavior is imitative.

Introduce one instrument at a time. Describe how the instrument is played correctly and what actions might cause damage. I emphasize that instruments are played lightly, and I avoid using words like "bang," "hit," or "crash" when describing how to play each one. Next, we pass the instrument around for each child to have a turn lightly tapping or shaking it. This is a highly motivating experience at the beginning of the school year, when some of the children are uncertain about participation. Many children will overcome their reluctance to participate when handed a special instrument to play. I encourage shy children to at least take the instrument and hand it to the next child.

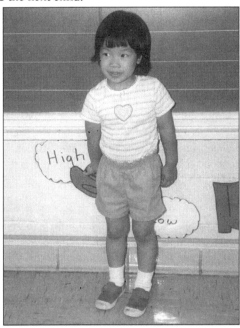

Student pointing to the icon for a high sound

After a variety of instruments have been explored, introduce the children to the signals that indicate when to begin and when to stop playing. The signals I use are: "instruments ready" (my hand is up and preparing to conduct) and "play" (I conduct in twos or threes), "instruments down" (I drop my hands, palms down, toward the floor), and "hands in your lap" (I hold my hands in my lap). Before distributing the instruments, I practice these signals until the children can perform the actions. After providing the students with instruments, I allow a few moments for children to explore sounds freely, occasionally interjecting the "begin" and "end" signals.

This activity may be followed by a lesson on loud and quiet. The children play as the teacher conducts or points to icons (pictures representing written symbols). This is also a good time to sing a song such as "Mrs. Parker Had a Band" (to the tune of "Old McDonald"), substituting instruments for the animals. The children only play on the chorus immediately after their instrument has been named. Subsequent lessons can introduce a simple timbre classification of skins (drums), wood (taps, shakes, and scrapes) and metal (jingles or bells). These classifications help the children understand how each instrument produces its sound.

By carefully reviewing the signals, reminding students about the correct way to play each instrument, and asking the students to classify their instruments each time they play, I ensure that instrument exploration time is meaningful as well as fun.

LISTENING

Guided listening is often a more difficult aspect of the music curriculum because of the prekindergarten student's short attention span. I find that music that tells a story or short character pieces are attractive to young children. Because of the child's lack of musical skills, the story element in this type of music is most appealing. Listening lessons can be enhanced by providing visual aids or by showing an actual object. Directing the children to close their eyes and imagine what the music puts on the "personal TV" can also help them focus attention.

Listening lessons should not be limited to playing a recorded selection while the children quietly sit. Invite children to signal changes in the music such as loud/quiet or fast/slow, to keep a steady beat with different parts of the body, or to stand and move to express the meaning of the music. Freely moving within a designated area is always fun with lively pieces. Whenever possible, listening activities should also include live performances in the classroom. The teacher or a guest can play an instrument or sing a song while the children practice good listening skills.

MOVEMENT

Rhythm and movement activities are important keys to enjoyment and learning during the full-group prekindergarten music class. At the beginning of the year, when attention spans are very short, the children need some kind of change in their activity every few minutes, and they need to have movement incorporated in every two or three activities. As the year progresses and the children mature, they are more able to concentrate on a continuous lesson idea for approximately half of the class time. This results in fewer needs for wiggle activities and perhaps only one gross motor movement experience toward the end of each class period. By providing quick breaks for the children to stretch or move, I control many of the "wiggles" without distracting from the actual lesson. For example, after finishing a song, I direct the children to remain seated and "touch your toes..., touch your back..., touch your head..., hands in your lap" while I turn on a record or make sure the instruments are ready for the next activity. This allows the children to have a brief movement break, and then they are ready to continue with the lesson.

If space permits, the children should be placed far enough apart that many of the movement activities can be at their established places. When a movement activity requires a larger space, this space should be carefully defined. Pieces of carpet are very effective for defining movement areas. The largest carpet is marked for the individual places and also becomes the boundary for some away-from place movement activities. If the activity requires an even larger space, the children can be spread around the room on other carpets. A carpet piece that is long and narrow is very helpful in defining space for "alley" movement activities so often used in familiar singing games.

Dances are often the prekindergarten student's favorite choice of gross motor activities. Many traditional dances can be simplified for the children. Again, providing boundaries for the movement and supplying the signals for starting and stopping will keep the fun under control. If a child is unable to dance nicely (and does such things as falling on the floor or pushing a partner), he or she is only allowed to watch as the class dances.

Music in ABA form or verse/chorus form works best for dances. Children might respond to the A (or verse) section with a more vigorous, individual movement and during the B (or chorus) section partners can be found to hold hands and dance around in a circle. Such experiences provide excellent practice for discriminating between large sections of the music and serve as an effective way to introduce children to musical form.

Finding partners for movement activities can be very chaotic if the movement is not carefully directed by the teacher. I invite the children to move one or two at a time when choosing a partner: When each child has selected a partner, the children are asked to sit in a specified place, facing one another, until everyone has a partner. To avoid the fuss over who's a friend with whom that day, it is wise to establish a rule stating, "If someone asks you to be their partner, you say 'yes.' " I reinforce appropriate behavior by calling students who are following the rules to choose partners first, and help the child who is always chosen last by calling his or her name first to choose a partner.

A POSITIVE ENDING

It is very important always to end with a quiet activity. Approaching this final transition creatively can help end the class on a positive note. One helpful idea is to instruct all of the children to "get into their boxes." They immediately curl up into little boxes, with knees under their bodies and hands covering their faces. By removing outside stimuli, I find that the children become quiet and ready to line up. I choose only the still, quiet ones to line up, and wait for others to comply. If a technique such as this is used consistently, the children soon learn the appropriate behavior for lining up. If at all possible, I have the children form the line at the door sitting down. Again, this is very helpful in reducing the number of problems that can develop when small children have to wait in line. The children are also ready to receive a personal reinforcer, if one is to be given. They can put their hands on their heads to receive a sticker, stamp, or award for good behavior. Always using the same hand for reinforcement helps the children learn to identify which hand is which.

By saving special chants or finger games for the lining up time, I find that the children remain attentive and orderly while waiting for their classroom teacher. For example, use a "Bumble Bee" chant from the lesson plan given earlier in this chapter. Being prepared with a specific plan for the important final minutes of the class makes the ending smoother and assures that everyone will leave with a happy memory of music time.

FOCUS ON CENTERS
by Holly Davis

My approach to working with children is based on these statements about early childhood education:
•Play is critical!
•Learning must be experienced!
•I hear, I forget; I see, I remember; I do, I understand!

My experience includes several years of experience teaching in a regular preschool classroom, and I have found that maintaining an approach that is based on the use of learning centers and adapting it to teaching music is very successful. Center time is by no means a "time-filler" to deal with the forty-five-minute class period; it is rather an extension of the lesson. Centers provide a special focus, giving important opportunities to develop concepts and build and practice social, motor, and thinking skills.

ROOM MANAGEMENT

Learning centers divide the classroom into smaller learning areas. They are arranged to provide ease of working and to promote a smooth traffic flow from one center to another. I use free student choice instead of teacher-directed movement during center time. I compute the number of centers needed by dividing the total number of students in class by three and adding that figure to the total number of students. (For example, fifteen students would need twenty centers.) This allows enough extra places for independent student choices and for movement from center to center. I also plan a place for full-group activity, with individual places that are designated by assigning each child a shape such as a flower, a square, a triangle, or a fish. These shapes are outlined in specific spaces on the floor with masking tape.

To help cut down on the amount of time needed to arrange the room for centers, I use a scaled-down outline of the room and pictures of furniture to arrange the centers and traffic areas on paper before actually undertaking the task. One must remember that the classroom arrangement should establish a place for materials and equipment and a sequence for some activities. This can be accomplished by using markings or pictures on shelves, boxes, trays, and directional charts, and an arrangement of games in sequence to suggest what needs to be done and in what order.

I use a classification system to analyze and evaluate the balance of center activities available in my classroom. This system provides information about each center that aids in planning a room arrangement. The categories in this system include:
•Noise level
•Size (number of places per center)
•Difficulty level
•Time required
•Maintenance/review of skills (Does the center involve practice of newly learned skills or practice to maintain established skills?)

CENTER MANAGEMENT

The child chooses his or her own order of participation in center activities. Each center has a reusable, color-coded sign that contains the name of the activity and one or more smiling face stickers: The maximum number of places available for that center is designated by the number of smiling faces on the sign and by the matching-colored clothespins attached to the sign. The children, sitting with legs crossed, hands in laps, and mouths quiet, are asked by the teacher to individually find a "key" (clothespin) in a center.

After clipping the key to his or her clothes, a child goes to the "center chart." This is a large chart on which the children mark their choices of the activities available to them for that day. The children's names and drawings of their assigned shapes are arranged down the side of the chart (each name beginning a row of boxes), and the name and icon for each available center appears at the top of the column of boxes (color coded to match the colors for the centers) for that activity. The child simply finds his or her symbol and name (the symbol is the same as the assigned floor shape) and traces a finger across the row on the chart. When the child finds the column that matches the color of the "key," he or she marks the appropriate box with a marker.

The child then goes to the center and interacts with the music materials. This procedure is followed until all of the children are busy in the centers. To change centers, a child clips the "key" back on the center sign's sticker, finds another center with a key, marks the chart, and proceeds with the new play.

A chart is maintained for each class, allowing the teacher to track each individual's use of the centers. Some centers will be available at any time, and some will be closed at certain times (such as when a teacher-directed activity is planned). I use a picture of an open or closed door attached with a rubber band to each center's sign, opening and closing them as needed.

The initial establishment of the centers involves a small expense. Almost everything I use, however, was made from discarded items (such as egg cartons or stocking "eggs") or was purchased at garage sales or discount stores. Centers do not have to be expensive unless you wish them to be.

CLASSROOM ROUTINE

One should direct the students in carefully taught routines before opening the centers for independent student use. My class routine is to greet the children at the door and, using various rhymes (for example, "Engine, Engine Number Nine"), to lead them around to their individual places. We all sit down and sing a hello song such as "Hello Everybody, Yes Indeed" and individual greetings, using a simple so-mi or so-mi-la melody, but without pressuring children to sing an answer. In September, we begin with rhythmically chanted name games such as "Who Is Sitting Next to You?" and then participate in a full group lesson followed by center time.

Care is taken that the children do not use materials and center areas incorrectly or unsafely.

The centers are introduced individually, and guided practice is used to reinforce correct procedures. I signal the end of center time by flashing the lights off and on again. We then clean up and "lock" the centers while singing a cleanup song. At the end of center time, we gather back together, each child seated on his or her own symbol space for closure. Closure involves a review of what was learned in the lesson and the distribution of reinforcers. I use stamps on hands, die-cut symbols, hand shakes, and hugs. We then line up by sitting down with legs crossed on the "line up tape" at the door.

EXAMPLES OF CENTERS

The following are examples of appropriate learning centers for four-year-olds. These plans include a summary of the objectives, materials, preparation, and procedures for each model.

Library Center (low-noise center for two people)

Objective: To provide children with the opportunities to develop and practice:

1. Thinking skills—by recalling stories or song sequences.

2. Visual and improvisational skills—by making up their own songs or stories to match what is seen in the pictures.

3. Language skills—by repeating songs or stories they have heard.

Materials: Song storybooks such as "The Little Old Lady Who Swallowed a Fly," music/musician storybooks such as Robert McCloskey's *Lentil* (NJ: Rae Publishing, 1978) or Thatcher Hurd's *Momma Don't 'Low* (New York: Harper & Row, 1984), or books of rhymes like *Mother Goose*.

Preparation: Obtain the books from the school library or personal resources, and place them in a special shelf area. Place a rug or pillow in the area to create a cozy reading environment.

Procedures: Emphasize the term "library" to reinforce understanding and use of school and public libraries. Teach the children that books may focus on musical ideas, and encourage them to sing rhymes or stories when appropriate. Arrange the center close to and across from the puppet center; participants can then become the audience for a puppet show or collaborate in a musical production of one of the library stories.

Listening Center (a low-noise center for four children)

Objective: To provide children with the opportunity to:

1. Explore and learn proper use and care of the tape recorder (as part of a listening station), tapes, and headphone sets.

2. Listen critically and carefully to retain musical information.

Materials: listening center (multiple headphone junction box), tape recorder, tapes, and headphones (books and manipulatives may also be included).

Preparation: Color-code the head sets to match the volume control knobs on the listening center; color-code the other important tape recorder controls with red for stop, green for play, and blue for rewind. Obtain prerecorded tapes or produce tapes of your

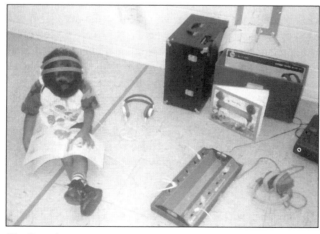

The listening center

own to go with stories, obtain or produce tapes of familiar songs, and acquire appropriate orchestral selections.

Procedure: Present procedures for use of the equipment in this center as a whole-group lesson. Emphasize that the children only touch the volume knob that matches the color of their headphones. Have each child correctly model the entire procedure of turning the equipment on and off. Provide any necessary explanation for the content of the recorded musical examples and interaction activities that are available.

Conducting Center (a high- or low-noise center for one person)

Objectives:

1. To use upper body movement to keep the beat.

2. To practice role-playing skills.

Materials: Conducting baton, tape recorder, prerecorded tape of march music, mirrored Con-Tact paper, and cardboard. To make this a low-noise center, supply headphones as well.

Preparation: Cover one side of the cardboard with mirrored Con-Tact paper and mount it on the wall to make a full-length mirror. Place tape player and baton in area.

Procedure: Model and monitor the use of the baton and other equipment as students demonstrate conducting in two. Encourage children to conduct the music and observe themselves in the "mirror."

Instrument of the Day (a medium-noise center for one person)

Objectives:

1. To explore sounds and demonstrate the proper use of simple instruments.

2. To learn about a variety of instrumental timbres.

3. To become aware that musical sounds can help express ideas and feelings.

Materials: Various rhythm instruments and materials, such as film canisters and rice, to make homemade instruments.

Preparation: Choose one kind of instrumental timbre to explore, such as rattling sounds (using homemade maracas). Create pictorial story strips that might use these sounds to help tell the story.

Procedure: Model and monitor correct use and care of the instrument or instruments. Encourage exploration of the sounds by asking the children to vary the speed or loudness of their playing. Place story strips in the area, and encourage the children to follow by verbally telling the story and inserting sounds at appropriate times.

CLASS BEHAVIOR MANAGEMENT PLAN

The fact that center time runs smoothly, with many children working independently, is due in part to the positive behavior-management system I have adapted and used. In this system, each class can earn rewards of "special activity time" (five minutes of the children's favorite musical activity) by exhibiting proper behavior. A giant music note, color coded for each class, is placed on a large staff chart. Good behavior advances the class note up the staff to the top line. After a class has reached the top, a star is placed on the note stem and the note is placed on the bottom line to begin the upward journey again. Notes are placed on lines, as the children are not yet ready for the concept of space. If a class demonstrates exemplary behavior, their note jumps up two lines as a bonus. Children enjoy being the "first" to the top of the staff.

Why does one undertake a program, based on the center approach, that entails this much planning and obviously consumes many hours of preparation? There is no doubt that this approach is age-appropriate, because the centers afford young children a freedom of choice and needed sense of controlling their play. Play is the most viable means to learning for this age child. I feel the center approach is essential because to a four-year-old child, the term "center time" means one thing: "I get to do it—I can understand it!"

Mollie Tower is the coordinator of elementary music in the Austin Independent School District in Austin, Texas. She has received national recognition for initiating the Music Memory Contest, voted as one of the one hundred most innovative curriculum ideas in the country. She has served as a consultant for basic textbook series published by both Macmillan and Holt, Rinehart & Winston.

Holly Davis is the prekindergarten through first grade music specialist at the Allan and Linder Elementary Schools in Austin, Texas. She has successfully taught in both private day-care centers and in the public schools.

Susan Carden Parker has taught music at the Brown and Brooke Elementary Schools at the prekindergarten levels in Austin, Texas. The topic of her master's thesis was in the area of early childhood music instruction.

The biannual Idea Fair, sponsored by the Brigham Young University Elementary Music Education Department, is a forum in which educators, parents, and community members can study ideas developed by students in the university's Music Methods for Early Childhood Education class. The fair provides students with the opportunity to display educationally and musically sound projects and build an educational network with the community.

CHAPTER 8

Reaching Out to the Community

by Susan Kenney

I f parents are the primary teachers of two- to four-year-old children, where do parents learn the connections between music and the very young? Where do day-care administrators and preschool teachers learn about music for preschool children? How can the university that trains primary and secondary teachers provide guidance to those who care for prekindergarten-age children?

Twice a year, at Brigham Young University, Elementary Music Education faculty members sponsor an Idea Fair where college students from all elementary music methods classes display ideas for stimulating music exploration with children. These displays include written music lesson plans, manipulative music objects for children to explore, music bulletin boards, and tape recordings of student-created songs and other activities for children with accompanying learning activities for teaching. Parents, public and private school teachers, and all interested community members are invited to browse, play with, and study the music education projects on display.

Before creating their projects, students in the Music Methods for Early Childhood Education class study developmental characteristics of children from two to five years of age, identify goals for musical growth, develop appropriate strategies, and observe their instructor teaching music to three- and four-year-olds at the campus preschool. Under the supervision of their instructor, they then apply the principles that they have been studying by teaching at the university preschool and helping organize and teach a four-week parent-toddler class.

To prepare for their projects, students may use materials available in the university's elementary music education resource lab. These materials include early-childhood music methods books, books on making homemade instruments and other music manipulatives, music textbook series, record collections, and photographs of projects completed by former students. Students are given written instructions that call for clear learning objectives, specific musical concepts the children will experience through the project, and developmentally appropriate teaching strategies. Child-centered strategies are encouraged. Specifically, students are asked to describe their prospective projects, to define the musical objectives of the project, and to list at least five learning activities that they might carry out with the project.

Once a student's project is approved, he or she may begin working. If the instructor has any concerns about a student's project, an individual meeting is scheduled to help that student bring the project into a clearer focus.

CONTACT: Susan Kenney, Brigham Young University, Department of Music, C-550 Harris Fine Arts Center, Provo, UT 84602

Staff members at the Education Department's media center have been very cooperative in helping students with tasks such as woodworking, metalworking, and painting. The Music Department has sent a set of resonator bells to the media center to help maintain the musical integrity of the instruments constructed there.

The Idea Fair is housed in the garden court of the student union building, a large, easily accessible room that can be locked at night. The room is reserved several months in advance. Rows of tables line the room, with hanging curtains or dividers behind the tables. The Early Childhood Music Methods class is combined with all other elementary music methods classes, thus creating approximately 175 projects for display.

In one corner of the room are a piano and chairs for chamber groups that perform throughout the day and evening. These groups are made up of music majors who volunteer their time during the fair. Not only do the music majors have an opportunity to perform, but their music provides an added experience for visitors from the community. In another corner is a "listening table," equipped with a tape recorder, where tapes from any project may be played. At the main entrance to the room, a student volunteer sits behind a small table to welcome visitors. Other students sit at each exit to answer questions and to insure against theft. Each student sets up his or her own project according to guidelines that specify display times and formats for the descriptions, exhibits, and handouts used in the projects.

Several weeks prior to the fair, the project's faculty coordinator contacts the university paper and the local paper; the papers write articles inviting the university community and public to visit the fair. Parents may bring children and may handle the projects to test children's interest. Some projects include handouts so that visitors can try the ideas or make their own projects at home. Students mingle in the garden court to answer any questions visitors may have.

While the projects are on display, the faculty and students grade them, identifying each project by an assigned number rather than by name. Each student evaluates his or her own project and those of three others (assigned by the instructor). Evaluations are based on four criteria:

Quality
Is the project neat, attractive, inviting to children?
Is the product free from rough edges, slivers, and so on, and safe for the age-group of children who would be using it?

Effort
Does the project reflect about twelve hours of *quality* work?

Usefulness
Are all parts (including mallets, if needed) present and functional?
Is the project musically sound: If it is a pitched instrument, are the pitches in tune? If it is a rhythm instrument, is the sound pleasing and enjoyable to the ear?
Are charts or other visual aids musically accurate? If visual aids are included, do they help the child grow musically?
Is the project appropriate for the age intended?

Educational value
Are the project's concepts and objectives stated clearly?
Are the learning activities clear to someone who has never seen them before? (Could another teacher or parent understand the suggestions and make the project work by following the written description?)
Will the use of this product increase the musical awareness of the child?
Are the teaching strategies developmentally appropriate for the age intended?

Students and instructors note a numerical score and written comments for each project. These evaluations are summarized to generate a final grade for each project. This gives students practice in evaluation, which will become an important part of their work as teachers.

EXAMPLES OF PROJECTS

Students in the Early Childhood Music Methods class are encouraged to consider the development of the whole child in the music activities they create. The following examples show teaching ideas that encourage cognitive, physical, and social or emotional, as well as musical, development.

Sound Blocks

Objectives: To help children describe sounds, categorize sounds, and use sounds to express ideas.

Description: Colored-fabric-covered cardboard boxes, with sounds inside. The sounds include two blocks with loud jingle bells, two with medium sound bells, two with soft bells, two with beans, two with rice, and two with salt.

Teaching ideas:

1. Encourage children to shake the blocks. Describe the sounds as loud or soft, ringing or rattling, and the same or different.

2. As children become familiar with the sounds, challenge them to find sounds that are alike.

3. Set two mallets in the environment with the blocks. Encourage the children to "play" the blocks with the mallets. Each box has a different sound and gives the effect of temple blocks when the children hit it.

4. Help the children group the blocks by color ("Bring all the blue blocks"), by timbre ("Bring all the ringing blocks" or "Bring all the rattling blocks"), by volume ("Where are the loud-sounding blocks? Where are the soft-sounding blocks?"), or by timbre and volume ("Where are the blocks with the loudest ring? Where are those with the loudest rattle?").

5. Encourage children to make towers of each kind of sound—that is, a tower of ringing sounds and a tower of rattling sounds. As a child knocks down the ringing sounds, play a triangle loudly to accompany the fall. As the rattling tower comes down, play the maracas to accompany the fall.

6. Shake the blocks to accompany singing. Help children make judgments about which sounds would be appropriate to accompany songs such as "Hush Little Baby" or "Jingle Bells."

Sound blocks

Slit drum

Slit Drum

Objectives: To allow children freely to explore sounds made from wood. To allow children to begin to feel a beat, to have a beautiful-sounding instrument to accompany singing, to use the sounds to tell stories, and to feel the joy of making high-quality sounds.

Description: A wooden box, measuring 6" x 7" x 17". The top side is cut to make four or more shapes of different sizes, which will create different timbres when struck with a mallet. The highest-quality sounds are created from hardwoods: The drum can be made by making five of the sides from pine and the top from hardwood. Hard rubber mallets, purchased from a music store, seem to bring the sounds from the wood in the most resonant way.

Music Tent: staff

Teaching ideas:

1. Set the drum and two mallets in the environment, allowing children freely to explore the sounds as they play.

2. Occasionally enter the environment, and describe the sounds a child is making as fast, slow, loud, soft, higher, lower. Compliment the child on his or her sound composition.

3. As a child becomes involved in the playing, play a duet with him or her on a rhythm instrument, Orff instrument, or recorder. If the child plays fast or slow sounds, try to imitate the rhythm. When the child plays fast sounds, play long sustained sounds. When the child plays slow sounds, you play faster sounds to complement the rhythms. If the child stops playing, you stop playing. When he or she begins again, you begin again. The child will soon discover that he or she is controlling the sound-making and will delight in trying to "trick" you.

4. Play the drum to accompany the singing of songs.

5. Play the drum with recordings of art music such as Ravel's *Bolero*.

Card Table Music Tent

Objectives: To provide a space away from distractions in which children are encouraged to explore improvisational singing, the playing of instruments, listening and moving to recordings, and the manipulation of musical notation.

Description: Four rectangular shapes of fabric are sewn together to make a tent that is closed on three sides when placed over a card table. The front side of the tent consists of two pieces of fabric made to look like curtains pulled back on either side. The following items are attached to the sides of the tent: (1) a picture of a town with a house, fire station, farm, school, store, park and connecting roads, and filled with singing people; (2) a set of pockets for holding instruments, songbooks, felt notation symbols, and so on; (3) a flannel-covered board with a musical staff; (4) scarves for dancing. The project also requires six stuffed fabric people; a set of large felt quarter, eighth, sixteenth, half, and whole notes; small picture books to use for singing stories; cassette tapes of music for listening and moving; and a recording of music featuring a piano, a trumpet, a violin, a bass viol, a drum, a guitar, and a clarinet.

Music tent: "Town"

Teaching ideas:

1. Place the rhythm instruments in the tent's pockets. Allow children to explore the sounds of the instruments. Describe the sounds played by the child with words such as loud, soft, fast, slow, clicking, ringing, or scraping.

2. Place a drum, triangle, wood block, and guiro inside the tent. Put the same instruments in the pockets outside the tent. When a child sits inside to explore the instruments, play the triangle from the pocket outside. Ask the child if he can find the instrument that makes the same sound. When the instrument is discovered by the child, have fun playing a triangle duet. Explore other sounds in the same way.

3. Place felt notes on the staff (mounted on the flannel-covered board). Allow children to manipulate the notes in any way they wish. Small children may throw the notes on the floor, then wait for you to replace them. As you join in this game, playfully name the notes when replacing them on the felt staff.

4. Older children may place the notes in higher and lower places on the staff. Ask them if you may "sing" the song they made; then improvise a song on "la." If the children are still interested, ask them what words would go with their song.

5. Take the family of fabric people from their pocket and walk them around the singing town. Improvise a story in song as you walk. When you come to the fire station, sing a "fire song"; when you come to the farm, sing "Old McDonald" or "The Farmer in the Dell."

Wooden music center

6. Place the tape recorder inside the tent. Allow children to push the buttons that turn the recorder on and off. If the children leave the music on for a time, describe the music they are listening to as loud, soft, smooth, jagged, staccato, or legato. Describe instruments that may be playing. As the children listen to the music, you can also encourage them to make the scarves dance.

7. Place a tape recorder inside the center with a tape of the following instruments: piano, bass viol, trumpet, drum, guitar. Place a set of Music Play musicians (described in Andress 1983, *Music Play Unlimited: Understanding Music Approaches for Childre n Ages 2–5, p. 9)* in the center and encourage children to listen to the music, determine which instrument is playing, and find the appropriate musician.

Wooden Music Center

Objectives: To provide a place where children may go to make choices about the musical activities in which they participate. Activities include ideas to stimulate listening, singing, playing instruments, moving to music, and creating.

Description: Four wooden walls are connected, with hinges, to a rectangular base. The walls create four centers that contain (1) instruments for free exploration; (2) a tape recorder with a tape of art music for movement, and scarves or streamers to use for dancing to the music; (3) books to encourage singing; and (4) wooden shapes attached to the wall with Velcro to encourage singing and chanting.

Teaching ideas:

The wooden music center functions in much the same way as the card table tent. A unique feature of the wooden center is the Velcro wall. The following ideas suggest ways to use that wall.

1. Help the children identify the wooden shapes on the board. Ask them to look for the cow and the moon. Sing "Hey Diddle Diddle" and help the cow jump over the moon in the appropriate place. Sing other songs such as "Mary Had a Little Lamb," "Ring Around the Rosy," or "The Farmer in the Dell," manipulating the pieces to tell the stories in the songs.

2. Make up song stories about the wood shapes, using freely improvised singing.

Musical Apron

Objectives: To provide awareness of musical symbols, to develop musical vocabulary, and to provide a stimulus for reviewing songs.

Description: The musical apron is an apron with several pockets. A felt music symbol is attached to each pocket with Velcro; instruments, cards with music symbols, or cards with pictures representing songs the children know are placed inside the pockets. The symbols on the pockets may be changed to expose the children to more music symbols.

Teaching ideas:

Each time a child takes something from a pocket, the teacher names the music symbol on the particular pocket, saying something like, "John took the sticks from the quarter note pocket."

1. Hide rhythm instruments in different pockets of the apron. Tell the children you have something hidden in your pockets. Encourage a child to come find something in one pocket; when an instrument is chosen, call it by name and allow the child to play that instrument in accompaniment to a class song. Continue allowing children to find instruments and to play them as the class sings.

2. Hide song titles in the pockets. Let the children choose songs to sing from the pockets.

3. Hide books in the pockets. Let children choose a book, then "sing" the book to the children, freely improvising a melody.

4. Ask children to find "sounds" in the room. When they find one, put it in the apron pocket. As the child places a sound in the apron, describe the sound as ringing, clicking, or scraping.

Musical apron

"Listen, Listen" Sound Game Song
Objectives: To encourage children to listen attentively and to begin describing sounds.
To help them sing and hear the interval of a major third.
Description: The "Listen, Listen" song and various musical instruments.

Listen, Listen

Lis - ten, lis - ten, what do you hear?   Lis - ten, lis - ten,   I   hear [*name*]

Teaching ideas:
1. Place maracas, a woodblock, and wrist bells in a place hidden from the child's view. As you sing, play one of the instruments, filling in the blank at the end of the verse with the name of the instrument being played. After playing the game a few times, allow a child to fill in the blank with the word that describes the sound. The child may want to trade places with the adult, letting the adult guess the instrument.
2. Play the game with other instruments such as piano, violin, or trumpet.
3. Find sound sources in the home such as pot lids, wooden spoons, typewriter, water running. Play the game blindfolded as sounds are made in the house.
4. Record household sounds. Sing the song, turning the recorder on to make a sound at the end of each verse.

5. Change the game and fill in the blank with descriptions of sounds such as "I hear ringing sounds," or "I hear clicking."

6. Choose several identical pairs of instruments or sound sources, and place one instrument of each pair out of sight behind a box. Place identical sounds in front of the box. Sing the song through once, playing a sound the child cannot see. Sing again, encouraging the child to match the sound he or she heard by choosing one of the instruments he or she *can* see.

Music Symbol Blocks

Objective: To expose children to musical symbols and vocabulary, to expand the musical vocabulary, and to describe events with sound.

Description: The music symbol blocks are fabric-covered foam rubber blocks, eight inches square, that have music symbols appliquéd to each side. Children may stack, throw, or sit on the light blocks without fear of damage.

Teaching ideas:

1. Encourage a child to stack or sit on the blocks. As the child plays, describe the blocks by color and musical symbols.

2. Play "can you find." With the child, search for a quarter note (or any other symbol) on the blocks. When you find it, act excited, saying "Look! I found the quarter note!" Together, look at the symbol, trace it, touch it, and keep repeating the word. Continue playing the game using other symbols. Do not expect the child to know all the symbols, and do not let this activity become a drill.

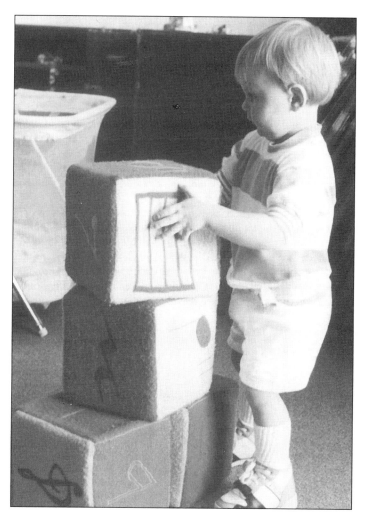

Music symbol blocks

3. Each time the child stacks the blocks and then knocks them down, play a loud drum sound as the blocks fall. Soon the child will notice the sound that he or she is creating and will try to determine whether the sound occurs every time the blocks fall. When the child finds that the sound will happen every time the block falls, he or she will want to play the game again and again. Encourage the child to play the drums while you stack the blocks. Timing the drum sound to the fall of the blocks is a delightful challenge for the young child.

4. Line the blocks up in a row on the floor or table so that one musical symbol is visible on each block. Ask the child if he or she would like to "sing" the music on the blocks. Freely improvise a song.

5. Line the blocks up as in number 4, and place an instrument in the environment. Invite the child to "play" the song on the blocks. Mix the blocks and ask the child to play another song.

Using musical stamps

Musical Stamps

Objective: To build musical vocabulary and awareness of musical notation.

Description: A set of rubber stamps (one such set is available from Musical Products, Box 20847, Milwaukee, WI 53220) and an ink pad.

Teaching ideas:

1. Tape a large piece of paper to the floor. Place a set of rubber stamps and a stamp pad on the paper. Allow children to stamp musical notes on the paper.

2. As children make notes on the paper, help them increase their music vocabulary by describing the notes as quarter notes, sixteenth notes, and so forth.

3. When a child makes a whole row of notes, ask the child if you can sing the song formed by the notes. Freely improvise a little song and compliment the child for his or her creation.

4. Place a rhythm instrument in the environment. After a child has stamped some notes, "play" the newly notated piece on the instrument. Compliment the child for his or her creation, and ask whether he or she would like to play the piece.

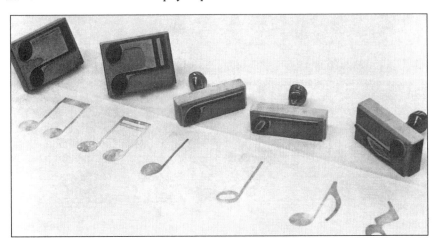

Students become teachers by teaching, and teachers increase their effectiveness by continued learning. At the Idea Fair, students teach a wide variety of musical activities. Knowing their work will be examined by peers, parents, and teachers, they work hard to create projects that are educationally and musically sound. Through the process, they learn to network with the community, an invaluable experience for those who go on to set up their own preschools or parent-toddler programs. Parents and teachers who attend can see, hear, touch, and feel innovative materials and study variations on traditional approaches to music education. Through the Idea Fair, the university can stimulate the imagination and expand the repertoire of musical activities and techniques for those who care for preschool–age children.

Early Childhood Music Books

Andress, B. 1980. *Music experience in early childhood.* New York: Holt, Rinehart and Winston.

Andress, B. 1983. *Music play unlimited: Understanding musical approaches for children ages 2–5.* Brown Mills, NJ: The World of Peripole.

Aronoff, F. W. 1982. *Move with the music.* New York: Turning Wheel Press.

Bacheller, J. 1975. *Music in early childhood.* New York: Center for Applied Research in   Education.

Biasini, A., R. Thomas, and L. Pogonowski. 1971. *MMCP interaction: Early childhood music curriculum.* Bardonia, NY: Media Materials.

Boswell, J., ed. *Young children and music.* Reston, VA: Music Educators National Conference.

Cohen, M. A., and P. J. Gross. 1982. Let's make music. *Parent's Magazine* (March), 52–57.

Faulmann, J. (1981). Montessori and music in early childhood. *Music Educators Journal* (May), 41–43.

Greenberg, M. 1979. *Your children need music.* Englewood Cliffs, NJ: Prentice-Hall.

McDonald, D. 1981. *Music in our lives: The early years.* Washington, DC: National Association for the Education of Young Children.

MENC Committee on Standards. 1986. *The school music program: Description and standards.* Reston, VA: Music Educators National Conference.

McDonald, D., and G. M. Simons. 1989. *Musical growth and development: Birth through six.* New York: Schirmer Books.

Moog, H. 1976. *The musical experience of the pre-school child.* Translated by C. Clarke. London: Schott.

Moomaw, S. 1984. *Discovering music in early childhood.* Boston: Allyn and Bacon.

Reilly, M. L., and L. Freeman Olson. 1985. *Time for music.* New York: Alfred.

Wharram, M., and F. Sweeney. 1979. *Song experience games for the very very young.* Portola Valley, CA: Richards Institute.

Music Textbooks

Boardman, E., B. Andress, M. P. Pautz, and F. Willman. 1988. *The music book.* New York: Holt, Rinehart and Winston.

Palmer, M., M. L. Reilly, and K. R. Scott. 1988. *World of music.* Morristown, NJ: Silver   Burdett & Ginn.

Staton, B., and M. Staton. 1988. *Music and you.* New York: Macmillan.

Child Development and Learning Environments

Bowen, E. 1986. Trying to jump-start toddlers. *Time* (7 April), 66.

Cahoon, O. W., J. M. Larsen, and B. J. Taylor. 1982. *To teach young children: Section 5. Patterns of child development.* Provo, UT: Brigham Young University.

Child choice—another way to individualize. 1987. *Young Children* (November), 48–54.

Gelman, D., S. Doherty, N. Joseph, and G. Carroll. 1986. The mouths of babes. *Newsweek* (December 15), 84–86.

Katz, L. G. 1980. Mothering and teaching—some significant distinctions. *Current topics in early childhood education.* Vol. 3., edited by L. G. Katz. Norwood, NJ: Ablex.

Singer, D. G., and T. Singer. 1978. *A Piaget primer: How a child thinks.* New York: Plume.

Wadsworth, B. J. 1984. *Piaget's theory of cognitive and affective development.* New York: Longman.

Musical Instruments and Other Creative Materials

Andress, B. 1983. *Music play unlimited*. Brown Mills, NJ: The World of Peripole. (Manipulative music toys for the very young).

Banek, R., and J. Scoville. 1980. *Sound designs: A handbook of musical instrument building*. Berkeley, CA: Ten Speed Press.

Hunter, I., and M. Judson. 1977. *Simple folk instruments to make and play*. New York: Simon and Schuster.

Kaplan, D. 1983. *See with your ears*. San Francisco: Lexicos.

Musical stamps. (Available from Musical Products, Inc., Box 20847, Milwaukee, WI 53220).

Sawyer, D. 1978. *Vibrations: Making unorthodox musical instruments*. New York: Cambridge University Press.

Wiseman, A. 1979. *Making musical things*. New York: Charles Scribner's Sons.

Recordings

Bowmar orchestral library series. Edited by L. Woods. Belwin-Mills. (Music for moving and listening).

Instruments of the orchestra. Conducted by H. Mitchell, National Symphony Orchestra. RCA Victor LE-6000.

The orchestra. Conducted by W. Babiak, narrated by P. Ustinov, Toronto Philharmonic. Mark Rubin Productions cassette MRP-107.

The small listener; the small singer; the small player. Edited by L. Woods. Belwin-Mills.

Susan Kenney is an assistant professor of music education at Brigham Young University and former national chair of the Society for General Music. She was an elementary classroom teacher for five years and a music specialist (K–6) for four years. She was co-chair of the Music in Early Childhood Conference (Brigham Young University, 1984), and has presented workshops in early childhood music education throughout the country.

Example projects by: Nancy Arnold (wooden center); Dixie Davis (slit drum); Sharla Dance (symbol blocks); Janet Holliday (card table); Alicia Locken (musical apron).

Curriculum planners must create activities that focus on music as an end in itself. Movement, which has a strong relationship with music, can be used in music and movement centers that try to achieve this focus. A high-quality stereo cassette player, appropriate props, and a teacher who describes, suggests, and models music-related movements can develop aesthetic perceptions in the preschool child.

CHAPTER 9

Music and Movement Environments in Preschool Settings

by Elayne Metz

The most important goal of music education is to develop students' ability to interact, with feeling, to the expressive elements of music. To achieve this increase in perceptions about music, one must listen and respond to all kinds of music, making more informed judgments as knowledge of the elements of music increases. Music has associations with other content areas, so it is easy to forget about the feeling of the music itself by being absorbed in its extramusical implications.

For example, a teacher may prepare a unit on food, in which the students sing a song about food and enjoy the experience very much. Some elements of the music may contribute to a pleasurable experience; since the focus is on food, however, we do not know what elements of the music elicit the children's response. In another situation, the voice on a recording sings directions for the children to stand up or sit down when they hear the name of a particular color, so that following these directions develops listening skills and color recognition. The whole process is more fun because the activity has taken the form of a song, but what has the child perceived about music through the experience? At the very least, the child might respond to the idea that music is fun, and the child may also respond to the beat of the music by clapping or bouncing, or he or she may like the sounds of the voices or the musical instruments used in the recording. The musical benefit derived from this activity, however, occurs more by chance than by design.

Simply using music in an educational setting does not insure that children's musical perceptions are developing. Creating activities for young children that focus on music as an end in itself is the goal of preschool curriculum planners. One activity that provides a visible response to what is being heard in the music is movement. The relationship between music and movement is strong: We say that music has "direction," or that the music "flows"; we describe the elements of music in terms of tension and release, or of pulling back and pushing forward. The body can actually represent many of the elements of music through movement, and as such is a useful tool in expressing music.

Movement is the child's first language, reflecting subtleties of thought and feeling not captured by verbal expression. The power of communication through movement is repeatedly

CONTACT: Elayne Metz, Arizona State University West, School of Music, Tempe, AZ 85287 seen in the play of young children. For example, an eighteen-month-old child responds with no prior instruction to a soft, slow instrumental selection by rolling up a blanket to use as a pillow, lying down on it with eyes closed, pretending to be asleep, only to jump up laughing a few minutes later. Without using language at all, the child has described the process of going to sleep as an innate response to sleepy-time music. Anyone who has observed a child's physical reaction to music knows that body movements tell much more about the child's feelings than could possibly be accomplished through the use of words.

MUSIC AND MOVEMENT CENTERS

Although the education component of a preschool program may vary from school to school, the format for learning tends to be similar. In many child-care or preschool settings, a special time is set during the day for specific learning activities. These activities, known as learning centers, are placed throughout the room, allowing the children to engage in self-initiated participation. Some of the traditional activities are the painting easel, the wet and dry table, blocks, and a book area. Often a particular craft activity relating to a theme will be offered. As children select a particular activity, teachers help where needed, moving from center to center. The learning center format makes sense in terms of the social and intellectual development of the preschool child, as described by Parten (1932), Piaget (1951), and Bruner (1960).

Social development: During the preschool years, from about two to five years of age, the child develops from a self-oriented to a social being. Mildred Parten (1932) described these changes in children's play as ranging from merely watching others play to engaging in cooperative play. Since children in a preschool classroom function on any or all of these levels of play at a given time, free choice participation in learning centers allows various levels of play to occur simultaneously. Providing a wide variety of developmentally appropriate learning activities demonstrates the awareness that children grow at different rates and possess changing interests and abilities.

Intellectual development: The preschool child's self-orientation can be seen in intellectual development as well as social development. Although the child has acquired the somewhat derogatory label of "egocentric," this attitude is the vital means by which a child learns about cause and effect. In the preoperational period (Piaget 1951) from about two to five years of age, a child has a tendency to center on only one dimension of a concept at a time, a form of thought known as transductive reasoning. For example, when the teacher gives a child a bean bag to move while listening to the music, the child may be drawn to the bean bag but oblivious to the music.

In creating experiences for the music movement center, teachers must find ways for children to center on the music itself. Activities might be presented in stages so that one element at a time would be introduced. Children might need a period of exploration and experimentation with materials before they hear the music. Suggested movements should lead the child to listen to the music. For example, a child may be asked to copy the teacher by touching various parts of his or her body while tapping the underlying beat of the music. A more effective activity, however, might be to have the children respond with just one movement in order to focus on the musical element.

The learning process: When creating music learning activities, teachers should consider the ways in which preschool children process their environment. Bruner (1960) identified three sequential stages through which a child progresses in order to understand ideas:

1. The enactive stage. In the enactive stage, the preoperational child represents concepts with body movement or manipulation of concrete objects. For example, a child can represent the sound of the long/short rhythm pattern by galloping.

2. The iconic stage. In the iconic stage, the child represents the same concept through a visual image. For example, the long/short rhythm pattern could be represented visually by a series of long and short lines.

3. The symbolic stage. The child uses arbitrary signs to represent experiences in the symbolic

stage. In this mode of representation, "galloping" rhythm pattern might be represented by a series of alternating quarter and eighth notes.

Since preschool children encode ideas primarily through the enactive mode of representation, body movement might be the principal means of musical understanding and expression at this point in their development.

Pitfalls to avoid: Early childhood music curriculum planners must apply the concept of the enactive mode of representation correctly. For instance, if a child hops on the lines and spaces of a staff drawn on the floor, it appears that the child is representing music through movement. In this case, however, what the child is representing through movement is the staff (a symbol that is part of the notational system of music) and not the music itself. The child's focus on the symbolic representation of pitch direction through the staff may actually interfere with the child's aural perception of pitch, making this an inappropriate activity for preschool children.

In the enactive mode, the concept of pitch representation might better be explored through activities in which children change their movement directions to indicate when they hear a change in a melodic idea or a change in pitch direction.

SETTING UP THE MOVEMENT AND MUSIC CENTER

To arrange the movement and music environment, clear a space in one corner of the room. Mark the area so that movement does not spill into other centers. Portable partitions can be made from colorful vinyl banners (about 5" by 8", with grommets in the top corners). Loop strong cords through the grommets and hang the banners from the ceiling with hooks, or fasten them to the ceiling frames used in suspended ceilings. Hang the banners at right angles, forming a space about 12" square with the two walls and the two banners. Children enter the area by walking between the panels. The important function of the banners as boundaries cannot be underestimated as it eliminates children becoming distracted, wandering around the room, or bringing chairs, books, and other objects to the music and movement center.

The area can be an appealing place that stimulates children to move. Since children love to watch themselves move, unbreakable mirror-backed Plexiglas panels provide that attraction. Plexiglas is lightweight and easy to move; it can also be attached to walls or framing (allowing it to be moved out of the space at the end of a session) with holes drilled in the corners of the panel. Two panels, each about 2" by 4" and placed in each corner of the area, seem to work well. Plexiglas scratches easily, so it must be stored carefully. Another item that stimulates children's movement is a revolving globe, made of small glass tiles, that is attached to the ceiling. When spotlighted in the darkened movement space, the globe emits wonderful moving spots on the walls and floor.

Sound system and recordings: A high-quality stereo cassette player should be placed in the area for each session. Good-quality recordings, representing various styles of orchestral and vocal literature, must be made available for movement experiences. Useful selections from the traditional music literature may include small character pieces for piano such as the Chopin *Preludes* or excerpts from Schumann's *Scenes from Childhood*. The march from Prokofiev's *The Love for Three Oranges* is an ideal piece for a brisk walking tempo, while the march from Tchaikovsky's *Nutcracker Suite* is a good example of accent in music.

When selecting music for children, a good rule of thumb is to play only recordings that you like yourself. Make sure they are in good condition and that the recording quality is up to modern standards. If the orchestration sounds old-fashioned or unappealing, look for another arrangement. For example, there are several versions of Walt Disney tunes on children's record labels, but the version with the original cast singing with full orchestral accompaniment provides a more musical listening experience.

When preparing taped examples for use in the movement area, selections can be recorded on continuous tape loops (of various durations) purchased in audio specialty shops. The use of the continuous loop eliminates the distraction and inconvenience of rewinding tapes during the session. Keep in mind that the length of the musical selection must be a little shorter than the length of the tape; it is not possible to tape over already recorded music. Using a stopwatch to check times before recording can avoid this problem.

Indiscriminate and discriminate use of props: It is common practice to provide objects as props in the classroom environment to motivate and enhance the child's movement play. What kinds of objects help children respond more expressively to music? At the Arizona State University West Campus setting (Metz 1986), we determined that objects should be provided for the children to use while moving to the music. Therefore, scarves of all sizes, colors, and shapes were placed in the area. Children used the scarves in every imaginable way, from tying them around their own necks to using them as blankets to wrap up a doll.

In other sessions, paper plates with yarn streamers were placed in the area: The children pretended that the plates were hats or wigs, but such objects did not appear to encourage movement related to the music heard. In fact, the objects appeared to detract from focusing on the music because of their *indiscriminate* use. The objects did encourage movement, but the movement did not reflect any specific quality of the music. We concluded that the object a child uses in moving to music has limited effect when possessing only generic associations. In order to increase musical perceptions, an object must reflect the more concrete association of a specific music idea with a specific body movement in order to increase musical perceptions. When objects are selected with this concept of *discriminate* props, the children's movement begins to focus on the music.

For example, if the children are to move to the song "Hickory Dickory Dock," they may adopt swinging as an appropriate gesture that represents the swing motion of the music. A discriminate prop for this music can be prepared by drawing a large grandfather clock on a poster, using a brass fastener to attach a cut-out pendulum to the picture, and hanging the poster in the music and movement center. Prepare a three-minute endless tape loop by recording the song yourself, accompanying your singing with claves "ticking" the beat. This homemade recording is preferable to a commercial one, since the children will enjoy recognizing their teacher's voice, and the ticking accompaniment emphasizes the beat.

Proceed by drawing the children's attention to the poster, encouraging them to move the pendulum back and forth while you sing the song. Invite children to imitate the movement of the pendulum by swinging their bodies to the music. As you describe their movements, you'll find them swinging not only arms but also legs and heads. "Hickory Dickory Dock" can be used in conjunction with a unit on time or on how machines work. Make a collection of different kinds of clocks; children can wind them up and listen to the ticking sound. A child may wish to chant or sing the Mother Goose nursery rhyme while holding the clock to his or her ear.

THE ROLE OF THE TEACHER

The role of the teacher is vital in the music and movement center. Our experience has shown that without guided interaction between student and teacher, the children's movements become undifferentiated in terms of music-related responses. The three most important functions a teacher can perform in the center are to *describe, suggest,* and *model.* Since children readily *describe* their own movements ("I'm going fast"), teachers can help to develop this movement vocabulary further by acknowledging and describing the children's movements. These descriptions also serve to stimulate other ways of moving. For example, if the teacher says "Danny's moving slowly," the statement will likely prompt Danny or others to move slowly. If the teacher notices someone swinging an arm, it may prompt more children to swing their arms or to swing another part of the body, thereby increasing a music/movement vocabulary and the children's creative fluency.

Suggesting is a technique designed to elicit specific movement responses from the children. Our experience has shown that almost all the children respond to the teacher's suggestions for movement. The teacher suggests movements relating to the music, thereby increasing the desired music-related responses of the children.

Modeling is a favorite activity of most children, who naturally imitate each other's movements and those of adults. Preschool children appear to copy the actions of their peers indiscriminately, however, making no observable distinction between movements relating to the music or another type of movement. When teachers model desired movements, children will increase music-related responses because of their insatiable urge to copy. Some children appear to be reluctant to imitate their peers or the teacher. (This is usually apparent in two-year-olds who are still developing social skills.) In our work, teachers found several opportunities to take the hands of these children and swing them side to side with the music, a technique referred to as *tactile modeling*. It appears that the younger the child, the more important tactile modeling becomes in influencing the disposition to participate in music activities.

STRATEGIES

Activities for the music and movement center are limited only by the needs, interests, and abilities of the children and the creativity of the teacher. The following classroom-tested strategies are included here only as models for new ideas. Some of the activities include extension into art and craft areas or other concept areas. Maintaining an attitude that is open to multidisciplinary influence will insure the continuing success of the music and movement area. Some ideas emerge from observing the natural movements of the children and creating music activities based on these movements. Other strategies follow from a given topic, such as Native American culture. Finally, some strategies grow from a favorite musical selection, especially those connected with children's literature.

The Blue Danube Waltz

Swinging and rocking are favorite movements of young children, and Strauss waltzes possess a compelling feeling of movement that even adults find hard to resist. Not only do children enjoy swinging their own bodies to this music, but they enjoy swinging dolls. For this purpose, stick dolls can be made by: (1) wrapping the end of a half-inch dowel (approximately 12" in length) with a ball of cotton, (2) covering it with a square of flowing silklike fabric, (3) securing the fabric square with a rubber band to form the doll head, and (4) using a marker to create a "smiley face" on the head. For safety, a large wooden bead should be glued to the opposite end of the stick to form a blunt end.

Children also enjoy having smiley faces marked on their fingers for "waltzing fingers." After these objects are prepared by the teacher or produced by the students as a project in the craft area, the children may take them to the music and movement center, where they can watch themselves swing to the Strauss waltz or any other compelling waltz music.

In modeling swinging movements, very young children may not be able to swing their arms in parallel motion because of an inability to cross the midline of the body. Thus, the teacher may need to model symmetrical arm movements. By three years of age some children will be able to swing arms in parallel action.

"Let's Go Fly A Kite"

When children move to this swinging song in triple meter, expect that they will probably swing in full circles, since there is more time between each accent than in a song such as "Hickory Dickory Dock." In the craft area, the teacher might cut tiny hand kites from tag board. Punch a hole in one end and attach yarn for a tail. Then staple a strip of tagboard on the back of the kite, forming a handle through which the children can slip their fingers. Children may assist by personalizing the kites with markers, stickers, ribbons, and so forth. Each child should have one kite for each hand. This helps them balance the body and promotes bilateral growth. Place a good-quality recording of "Let's Go Fly a Kite" from the musical *Mary Poppins* in the music and movement area. Encourage movement exploration by asking the children what their kites are doing, and model circular movements to encourage the extended feeling of this song's meter. This activity can be enriched by taking a real kite outside on a windy day. Invite children to move their bodies the way the real kite moves in the sky.

GALLOPING

This is another locomotor movement that stems from the natural actions of the child. Between the ages of two and three years old many children attempt galloping, a movement that develops at an earlier age than skipping. Both galloping and skipping are repetitions of a rhythm pattern of one long and one short sound. In the gallop, the same forward foot always responds to the long sound; in skipping, alternate feet respond to the long sound. Some locomotor movements are easier than others to synchronize with music because gravity determines their performance. In galloping and skipping, for example, gravity controls the speed at which the body returns to the ground after the initial leap. On the other hand, in a movement to a steady beat such as walking, the speed of all the steps is determined primarily by self-control of body movement.

Educators have a tendency to begin rhythmic studies with a steady beat, since it is the fundamental pulse of all rhythm. In *physical* responses to music, however, movements that depend on gravity may be preferred as first locomotor activities associated with music because they can be performed more accurately by a small child than can movements determined by conscious control of the body. (In addition, the steady beat has no differentiation of sound, causing difficulty in tracking the occurrence of each sound. When sounds are organized into regular rhythm patterns and meters, the body can follow along more easily.)

Galloping may then be preferred over stepping the beat as a first locomotor activity, so the teacher may wish to plan activities such as the following:

1. *Prepare or help children prepare* hand-held horses (two per child). This can be done by cutting horse silhouettes from tag board. Yarn, paper, or foam manes may be glued on; the eyes, nose, and mouth can be drawn on with a marker. Attach the horses' heads to tongue depressors or other blunt-edged sticks that are approximately 6" in length.

Prepare a cassette tape of galloping music by improvising your own music or by using a recording. Be sure to gallop to the music yourself to see whether the rhythm and tempo are correct. If the music is too fast for you, it should be just right for the legs of small children.

When children are responding to the music, model and describe the children's movements, encouraging them to prance high. Suggest that in each hand they hold a horse, which will balance the body and lift the arms, helping the child to achieve high movements. While children are galloping, suggest that they put their "unfavorite" foot forward to develop bilateral growth, which ultimately leads to the skipping movement created by alternating feet. Put inverted egg cartons, with small holes in the bottom, in the music and movement center. These cartons can act as the "horse barn" where children can put their horses when not in use.

2. *Dancing bells* are the basis of an activity that incorporates elements of the Native American culture into the preschool music program. (A word of caution: Before adapting unfamiliar cultural customs for music strategies, you must research those customs in reference works or seek out persons from that culture who are available in your area. Some songs, dances, and materials may only be used in religious ceremonies by the members of a culture, and some customs, carried out only by adults, would be inappropriate for preschool children.)

Many Native Americans wear dancing bells or jingles around their waists or ankles when they dance. Preschool children can make their own dancing bells by stringing jingle bells on an elastic band. A stiff "needle" for threading the bells can be created by tightly wrapping a short piece of tape on one end of the elastic band. After the bells are strung, the tape is removed and the ends are tied together to form a leg or waist band that can be easily put on and taken off by the child. In the music and movement center, play a cassette recording of authentic Native American dance music representative of the tribes in your state or other geographic locations.

The jingling bells serve the purpose of drawing attention to a particular part of the body. Children will probably pick up their feet and move at the waist in order to sound the jingles. Some Native American dances are just for males or females, but your class need not be limited by this fact. You might simply mention that in the original culture this is a boy's (or a girl's) dance, and then allow all the children free access to the dance.

Boy's Fancy War Dance

Traditionally, men or boys wear "shags," pieces of wool tied around the ankle to protect the skin from the jingles. Shags can be made with mock wool fabric with a piece of cord woven lengthwise through the center and tied around the ankle. Jingles can be tied over the shag or put on the shag as the cord is woven through. A headband can be made from a strip of bright fabric stitched to a piece of elastic. Children can make their own paper feathers to slip in the back of the headband.

One of the skills of the Fancy War Dance is to be able to stop dancing exactly when the music stops and to start again when the music starts. Adapt this idea to the music you have available. When making the tape for the music and movement center, include 10–20 seconds of silence between phrases or sections. The dancers then move when the music starts and stop when the music stops. The steps and motions can be improvised, based on moving those parts of the body that can make many jingling sounds.

Boy's Shield Dance

While dancing, Native American males traditionally carry shields painted with signs from nature or pictures of meaningful dreams. Children can make their own shields from paper plates. Cut a strip of tagboard and fasten it to the back of the plate as a handle. Children can decorate the "shields" with their own designs.

When dancing, the child can hold the shield in one hand and a handmade rattle in the other hand. The child will have great fun with the variety of sounds and moves to be made with the jingles, rattle, and shield.

Girl's Fancy Shawl Dance

Women usually dance with a shawl around the shoulders and feather fluffs in the hair. Simple shawls can be made with a piece of fabric (about 3" by 1"; add fringe if desired). Individual fluffs can be made with a few small down feathers bound with a string and attached to a hair clip. These props can be placed in the music and movement area and used when dancing to the music.

In these examples, the steps and motions are improvised by children in response to the music; no attempt is made to teach a child the authentic shawl-dance steps. This activity provides children with an opportunity to interact with Native American music and to become aware of some of the costumes and objects important in the dances associated with this music.

Music educators must not merely view body movement as an enjoyable accompaniment to music activities: They must recognize it as an essential tool for developing musical perception in young children. Movement is a primary means of expression in preschool children, so music educators must observe and interact with children in natural settings in order to understand how movement represents feelings and ideas. Tapping the expertise of preschool teachers and care givers who have firsthand, daily experience with the developing physical needs, interests, and abilities of the young child will contribute greatly to the music educator's present resources.

Many administrators of preschool and day-care facilities welcome visits to the school. Observation of any activity (including nap time) will yield powerful insights into the function of movement as an expressive language. Once the natural movements of the child are observed, one should consider how those movements might be associated with a particular musical element or piece of music. Often, educators select activities based on a musical idea or song they wish to teach instead of creating a music strategy that coincides with the child's frame of reference. Changing from a teacher-based to child-based instructional focus will strengthen the preschool music program. Music educators and early childhood educators working together may stimulate the linkage of music and movement as an ideal medium for developing aesthetic perceptions in the preschool child.

References

Bruner, J. 1960. *The process of education.* New York: Vantage.

Metz, E. 1986. Movement as a musical response among preschool children. Doctoral diss., Arizona State University, Tempe. *Dissertation Abstracts International,* 47, 3691.

Parten, M. 1932. Social participation among preschool children. *Journal of Abnormal and Social Psychology* 27, 243–369.

Piaget, J. 1951. *Play, dreams, and imitation in childhood.* New York: Norton.

Elayne Metz is an assistant professor of fine arts at Arizona State University West Campus. She is also a licensed instructor of Dalcroze Eurhythmics, a method of teaching music through body movement. Her research focuses on movement as a musical response among preschool children, a topic that she has presented at many national and regional conferences and clinics. She is recipient of the Burlington Northern Foundation Faculty Achievement Award.

Teachers can prepare children to participate in creative activities by teaching them the "wherewithal" for these activities. Giving children a reservoir of knowledge and skills for moving creatively to music and understanding music can help them in the process of expressing themselves imaginatively.

CHAPTER 10

Musical Understanding Through Creative Movement

by Leon H. Burton

T here are three popular themes today that relate to the educational needs of young children. If all the themes were identified and placed in order of priority, creative imagination and expression would be near the top of the list. The need to foster creativity has long been recognized as important at all educational levels, particularly in early education. But the problem of what to do in the classroom with children to encourage and stimulate creative thought and action has often resulted in a lingering fuzziness that leaves many teachers with unanswered questions.

What is creativity? Can creativity be taught? How do I proceed to involve young children in creative activities? There are ways in which teachers can prepare children to participate in creative activities, and there are guidelines for using creative movement as a vehicle for developing and reinforcing understanding in music.

SOME THINGS RESEARCHERS SAY ABOUT CREATIVITY

Researchers report that creative imagination peaks in young children at about the age of 4 ½ years and then begins to decline. The decline is generally attributed to such things as (1) social pressures that constantly remind children to be realistic and stop imagining, (2) approval of only those behaviors that follow established traditions, (3) learning environments that cause children to be fearful of trying a new approach, (4) strict control that limits or prohibits questioning and exploration, (5) too high a value placed on conformity, (6) overemphasis on memorization, and (7) too many rigidly planned tasks.

Learning environments that stimulate creative imagination are generally described as providing opportunities to (1) contribute original ideas, (2) share differing points of view, (3) seek new ways to look at problems, (4) fantasize, (5) develop research and inquiry skills, and (6) participate in learning activities where there is a feeling of trust and equality. Researchers also point out, however, that too little stress can result in children having difficulty focusing on problems, and too much stress can generate a sense of rigidity.

Research also reveals that there is a direct relationship between the development of a person's creative ability and the likelihood of that person becoming a fully functioning, mentally

CONTACT: *Leon H. Burton, Curriculum Research and Development Group, Education Department, University of Hawaii, Honolulu, HI 96822* healthy, well-educated, and vocationally successful individual. Children, therefore, need to be confronted with appropriate challenges at a very early age. They need to explore the use of thinking skills and must not be taught to take only conventional approaches to finding solutions to problems.

But what is creativity? Have you ever attended a workshop or some other kind of educational activity and been asked to find a space to move creatively in response to music? If so, how did you know whether your movements were creative? Or have you ever been asked to move creatively to depict an animal or person having certain characteristics? If so, were your movements creative? And how do we know whether we, as teachers, are engaging children in creative activity or in activity that lacks creative elements? The answer lies, perhaps, in what creativity is and how creative imagination is developed.

THE TEACHING OF WHEREWITHAL

Can creativity be taught? Some believe that children cannot create unless they have the "wherewithal" for creation. Consider for a moment what this might mean in relation to our own creative abilities and those of the children we teach: Wherewithal suggests the need for acquiring knowledge and developing skills that can be used in the creative process. A young child, for instance, may participate in a drawing activity using only the point of a pencil. The child's previous experience may not have opened the possibility of shading in drawings (knowledge), and that shading can be achieved by holding a pencil in a different position and using varying degrees of pressure (skill) to achieve different intensities. But by acquiring new knowledge and developing new skill, children have acquired new wherewithal that opens up a greater range of possibilities for creative expression. Wherewithal can be taught.

A child may not have previously used a shimmering body motion to respond to music that suggests such movement. And the child may also have never developed a keen awareness of the use of force (strong, light, smooth, or percussive) in movement to reflect changing degrees of loudness and rhythmic activity in music. As the children learn to recognize varying degrees of loudness and rhythmic activity in music (knowledge), and use shimmering movements (skill) that correspond with the levels of force suggested by music, they have acquired new wherewithal to use in creative activity. Again, wherewithal can be taught.

WHAT IS CREATIVITY?

Creativity is a process of combining known factors (knowledge, skills) in new ways to produce new results—a new product, a new way of thinking and perceiving, a new way of performing. As teachers, we need to provide children with an ever-expanding reservoir of knowledge and skills (wherewithal) and establish learning environments that will stimulate creative thought and action. This definition implies that the educational process is important to the development of creative imagination. The more knowledge and skills that children acquire, the better equipped they become to think creatively and to use what they have acquired in creative ways.

The definition also implies that creativity is "more than" the creation of some kind of product. It is also a process of using our acquired knowledge and skills in new ways to think through possible solutions to problems and to perceive things in new ways. A musical performance can be a creative experience for a listener; an art exhibit can be a creative experience for a viewer; a dramatic production can be a creative experience for those who observe what they see and hear using creative skills; an office worker can go about organizing details and procedures in a creative way to make what would normally be dull, routine work become more interesting and satisfying. Creative thinking can and should become an integral part of every aspect of our lives. The goal for early education teachers should be to help each child develop to an optimum level the ability to think and act creatively in all aspects of life.

MOVEMENT WHEREWITHAL FOR YOUNG CHILDREN

Children who develop skill in moving their bodies in a variety of ways and learn to differentiate between kinds of movement will have a greater repertoire (wherewithal) from which to choose when asked to move creatively to music. Early education is a time to help every child learn to move his or her body in a variety of ways and to name as many of the movements as possible. Each child needs to learn the following basic movements: jumping, leaping, hopping, walking, running, skipping, crawling, stalking, galloping, sliding, slithering, shimmering, swinging, swaying, collapsing, twisting, bending, stretching, jerking, turning, and spinning.

Over time, one should help each child learn to move in each of the ways listed (and in other ways you may wish to demonstrate and name). After they have learned some of the movements and can name them, you might have the children move in response to your instructions such as "Jump three times"; "Hop five times"; or "Run until I tell you to stop." Tapping a drum or clapping your hands can serve as a valuable sound source to indicate when to begin moving, how fast to move, and when to stop. All the children should learn eventually to move in each of the ways as you call the names of the movements. This is a valuable exercise because it requires recall, execution in response to sound, and both small and large muscle coordination.

Use of space: When the different movements have been learned—or as they are being learned—other aspects of movement can be introduced and demonstrated. Children can be assigned a space for a stretching activity and can be asked to explore the use of levels (high, medium, low) as they move their bodies. They can also be asked to explore the use of movements that imply size change (wide, narrow, large, small). Direction is another use of space: The children can be asked to use a sliding movement in forward, backward, sideward, and circular directions, reversing the sideward and circular directions on signal.

Use of shape: As children develop an understanding of the use of space in movement, they can begin to use their bodies to form representational shapes (such as those of a fork, balloon, or cup), geometric shapes (such as squares, triangles, or circles), and abstract shapes.

Use of force: Children also need to learn to apply different levels of force in their movements. Strong and light running, percussive jerking, and smooth turning could be used to teach and illustrate the use of force in movement.

Movement in relation to time: This is a very important aspect of movement since it applies directly to music. Walking, hopping, twisting, swaying, and performing other movements to a steady beat is a skill essential to children's later musical development. This could be done while listening to selected recordings of music, to steady drum taps, to steady hand claps, and to other sources of sound that keep a steady beat. Running to beats that alternately become faster and slower can help children grasp the idea of tempo (speed of the beats). A rhythm pattern such as pattern *a* in the accompanying figure can be learned by first clapping it and then moving to it with jump-jump-jump motions. Movement to pattern *b* could be learned by clapping it and then stepping it twice, first forward and then backward. The rhythm pattern *c*, with an accent on the last beat, could be learned first by clapping and then by illustrating it with jerk-jerk-jerk motions.

Rhythm patterns

As the children progress in their ability to execute movements to the beat and to rhythm patterns, have them begin using several different movements for one pattern. The following figure shows a few examples you might use before you begin to create your own. When the

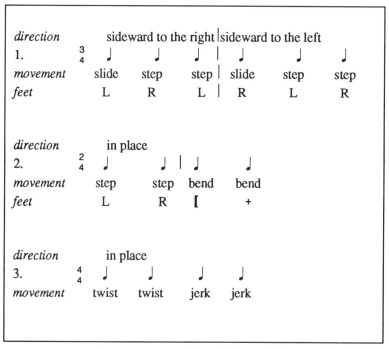

Movement patterns

children have developed the ability to use several different movements for a particular pattern, you might find short recorded selections of music that could be used for the different patterns (for example, a slow waltz for the first movement pattern, a march for the second pattern, a slow blues or jazz piece for the third pattern). The goal is to have the children continue repeating the pattern to the beat for the duration of the music. An additional long-range goal is to have them listen to a new piece of music and individually create patterns of movement to respond to what they hear. They may eventually create other patterns that include movements alternating with body and mouth sounds.

The creative process of thought and action implied by these activities is possible only in learning environments that give children the freedom to explore and experiment (which is different from nondirected activities that can lead to chaos). The initial creative attempts of young children will often not appear to be creative at all. But as more opportunities are provided, the children will begin to achieve refinement both in their abilities to experiment and in their actual movements.

MUSIC WHEREWITHAL FOR YOUNG CHILDREN

Young children will develop a lifelong interest in and appreciation for music only by learning to understand what music says "as sound," and acquiring wherewithal is essential to building understanding. Recordings of music played at different intervals in the child's school day, sing-alongs, and singing-movement games are all valuable vehicles for musical experience, but when used in only general ways (without focusing musical understanding), they fail to equip young children with the knowledge and skills they need for future musical growth.

Wherewithal is best acquired as children experience music and are helped to focus on some aspect of what they have heard. The musical experience becomes the basis for developing understanding and related skills. Verbalized explanations of music have meaning for young children (or adults) only in relation to the musical sound they have experienced. It is the musical sound, then, that must serve as the departure point for acquiring wherewithal.

The brief activities that follow include activities for the development of wherewithal in music appropriate for presentation to young children. The activities are written, however, with full recognition of the limitations written words have when represented without the benefit of musical sound. Incorporated into the activities are suggestions for movement, but if the children can think of other ways to move to illustrate the same musical idea, then encourage them to do so.

The characteristics of sound: There are four characteristics of sound that are important in developing aural awareness. These are pitch, loudness, duration, and timbre. Young children need many repeated experiences both in producing sounds while focusing on these characteristics and in recognizing the characteristics in sounds produced by others. The activities that follow may suggest the creation of other activities and patterns of movement that will help the children develop skill in recognizing these characteristics.

Pitch

1. Have the children sing the word "high" several times using the highest voice sound possible while making their bodies tall and extending their arms upward. Then have them sing the word "low" several times using the lowest voice sound possible while bending their bodies over with their arms dangling.

2. Sing or play several higher and lower pitches on an instrument such as piano, resonator bells, or recorder, and help the children develop a sense of relative highness and lowness for the sounds they will hear. Then play or sing single higher and lower pitches and ask the children to use their bodies (in creative ways, of course) to show their recognition of higher and lower sounds. Introduce the word "pitch" when you believe it is appropriate.

Loudness

1. Have the children sing the word "loud" several times while moving their bodies in ways to suggest loud. Then have them sing the word "soft" several times while moving their bodies to suggest soft.

2. Play a recording of music and ask the children to move about the room in ways to indicate their recognition of louder and softer. You should adjust the dial that controls the volume level of the record player or tape deck during the activity to make the music louder and softer in a very obvious way. Introduce the word "loudness" when you believe it is appropriate.

Duration

1. Have the children sing the word "long" (using a long sound) several times while taking long, slow steps. Then have them sing the word "short" several times while taking short steps.

2. Use your voice or an instrument to produce longer and shorter sounds and ask the children to take longer and shorter steps in response to what they hear. Introduce the word "duration" when you believe it is appropriate.

Timbre

1. Have the children produce sounds with hand claps, foot stomps, tongue clicks, thigh taps, and lip pops, and then have them tell whether the sounds were alike or different. Help them learn to name and differentiate between the sounds by the ways the sounds were produced.

2. Play several rhythm instruments (such as tambourine, triangle, wood block, or rhythm sticks) and help the children learn to name and recognize each by sound. Then play each instrument—one at a time—behind a barrier of some kind, and invite individual children to go and identify the instrument heard. Each child should move in a way different from the previous child (reinforcing creativity) as they go to identify the instrument. The instrument should be held up by the child so that others can verify whether the correct instrument has been identified. Introduce the word "timbre" when you believe it is appropriate.

Patterns of sound: Combining pitch, loudness, duration, and timbre in various ways produces patterns of sound. The following activities will help young children begin to develop some understanding and skill in identifying them.

Melody

When children sing songs, they sing a succession of pitches of varying durations that together make a melody. Melodies rise and fall in pitch and sometimes have pitches that are repeated.

1. Have the children sing a song they know well and, with their arms extended in front of them, ask them to move their hands to trace the melody's upward and downward direction. Introduce the word "contour" when you believe it is appropriate.

2. Have the children sing a song, such as "This Old Man" or another simple song, using very short sounds while producing short body movements. Introduce the word "staccato" when you believe it is appropriate.

3. Have the children sing "Twinkle, Twinkle, Little Star" or another simple song and produce long, smooth sounds while using long, smooth body movements. Introduce the word "legato" when you believe it is appropriate.

Rhythm: The beat or pulse of music is one of the aspects of the organization of sound that most strongly attracts the interest of young children. Longer and shorter sounds used to form rhythm patterns establish rhythmic ideas that we can recall and reproduce.

1. Play a recording of a march and ask the children to use their bodies to show you the beat of the music. They could move about the room or remain stationary while moving body parts. Introduce the word "beat" when you believe it is appropriate.

2. Play slow, steady beats on a drum and ask the children to move their bodies in response to what they hear. Then play steady beats at a faster speed as the children move. Alternate playing steady beats at faster and slower speeds as the children move their bodies to reveal their recognition of different tempos. Introduce the word "tempo" when you believe it is appropriate.

3. Ask the children to sing a simple song that is very familiar to them. Afterward, select a short rhythm pattern from the song such as ♪♪ ♩ from "This Old Man" and have the children clap it. As one group sings the song again, a second group could move their bodies to the selected rhythm pattern, repeating the pattern until the song ends. Introduce the words "rhythm pattern" when you believe it is appropriate.

Form: Young children must begin developing an awareness of parts of musical selections that sound the same and parts that sound different.

> Select a song that is familiar to the children and has a verse and a chorus. Ask one group of children to clap their hands to the beat for the verse and a second group to move in some creative way to the beat of the chorus. The goal is for the children to use movement to help in distinguishing between these two large parts of the song. Short, recorded selections could also be used for this purpose. Introduce the word "part" when you believe it is appropriate.

Texture: Texture in music describes the functions of different sounds and whether the sounds are heard one at a time or more than one at a time.

> 1. Ask the children to sing "Are You Sleeping" while walking in place to the beat. Help them realize afterward that they were singing and moving in unison (all singing and moving in the same way at the same time). Introduce the word "unison" when you believe it is appropriate.
>
> 2. Have one group of children sing "Are You Sleeping" as a second group sings the entire song on one pitch. Ask the first group to walk in place as they sing; as the second group sings the one pitch throughout, they can move their arms and heads in creative ways to contrast with the first group's movement. The second group's musical function is to provide a pleasing accompaniment to the first group. Point out later that they did not sing in unison. Introduce the word "accompaniment" when you believe it is appropriate.

Tonality: All of the songs that young children sing have a pitch around which all of the other pitches tend to gravitate. In many instances this will be the last pitch of a song, and in other songs it will be both the first and the last pitch. The pitch is also likely to be prominent at different points in a song.

> 1. Have the children sing a simple song such as "London Bridge." As they sing the song a second time, they should exclude the last pitch (on the syllable *dy).* Help the children realize how they like to sing the last pitch ("home tone" or "tonic") because it creates a sense of finality or completeness. As the children sing other songs—and their ability to recognize the tonic pitch improves—ask them to strike a pose or move in some unique way each time they hear the tonic. Introduce the word "tonic" when you believe it is appropriate.

Harmony: As resonator bells, Autoharp, piano, guitar, or some other pitch-producing instrument is used to play chordal backgrounds to songs, the different pitches sounding together produce harmony.

> 1. Have the children sing a song that is familiar to them. Then, using an instrument such as an Autoharp, strum a chordal accompaniment as the children sing the song again. The goal is to help them recognize when pitches other than those they are singing are sounding at the same time. To reinforce their recognition of the simultaneous sounding of pitches, sing a song several times while alternating between singing with and without the accompanying instrument (the instrument you play should be hidden behind a barrier, out of sight of the children). Ask the children to move creatively when they hear pitches (the sounds of the instrument you play) together with those you are singing and to remain stationary when you are singing without the accompanying instrument. Introduce the word "accompaniment" when you believe it is appropriate.

Although these suggested activities use movement to aid in recognition of specific aspects of music, children also need opportunities to respond in a general way to music without focusing on specifics. Provide opportunities for them to move creatively to entire songs and recorded instrumental selections. You can observe their movements and discuss them later as a means of revealing their impressions of the music they heard.

Creativity in movement and music is not unlike creativity in other subject areas. The more children know about something—and the more skills they develop in using what they know—the greater the likelihood they will further develop their creative abilities. Children need to learn how to move in a variety of ways to "free their bodies" and build a reservoir of wherewithal to use as a resource in the future. Movement is fun for children, and when used properly it can be an excellent tool for expanding and reinforcing children's understanding of music and sound.

Children develop understanding in music only when they acquire the wherewithal essential to understanding, which forms a base from which creative thought and action in music can spring forth. For instance, with a knowledge of tempo and contrast, children could use rhythm instruments to create sound patterns that are performed at different tempos and alternate speeding up (accelerando) and slowing down (ritardando). A recording of the children's creation (or composition) could be made and then used later for a movement activity. With a knowledge of rhythm patterns, the children could create a sound piece that consists of a rhythm pattern they have created and then performed using rhythm instruments or sound sources of contrasting timbres. Contrasting levels of loudness could be added to the piece.

Creativity is a process. It is the process of learning and then using what has been learned to express oneself imaginatively in new ways. We, as early education teachers, should make every effort to keep creative imagination alive; we should not let it peak at age 4 ½ and then begin a decline. Finally, we, too, should become creative in our work. Our creativeness just might become contagious among the children we teach!

Leon H. Burton is a professor of education with the College of Education's Curriculum Research and Development Group, University of Hawaii. He is project director of the Hawaii Music Curriculum project, which has produced a sequentially and conceptually organized K–12 instructional program in music, and is currently project director for early education program development. He is author of several early education publications which focus on art and drama, as well as music learning activities for young children.